LEET WATER FROM SOURCE TO TWEED
WHITSOME TO SWINTON TO COLDSTREAM

Also by Antony Chessell

The Life and Times of Abraham Hayward, Q.C., Victorian Essayist 'One of the two best read men in England' Lulu Publishing 2009

Ed., *A Small Share in the Conflict; The Wartime Diaries and Selected Correspondence of Flt Lt Henry Chessell (R.A.F. Intelligence Branch)* Lulu Publishing 2009

The Short and Simple Annals of the Poor; Some Family Ramblings Lulu Publishing, 2010 private circulation only

Coldstream Building Snippets Cans, Quoins and Coursers Lulu Publishing 2010

The Braw Trees of Coldstream Lulu Publishing 2011

Ed., *The Sixpence That Grew and other Antony Trumpington Stories*, Avis M. Chessell Lulu Publishing 2011 private circulation only

LEET WATER FROM SOURCE TO TWEED

WHITSOME TO SWINTON TO COLDSTREAM

Antony Chessell

Foreword by
Major-General Sir John Swinton, KCVO, OBE

Published by Lulu

First published in 2012

Lulu Enterprises UK Ltd., 7 Crooksbury Road

Farnham GU10 1QE www.lulu.com/uk

Copyright © Antony Chessell 2012

Antony Chessell asserts the moral right to be identified as the author of this work

A catalogue record for this book is available from the British Library

ISBN 978-1-4477-2511-4

Typeset in Times New Roman

Printed and bound in Great Britain

Front cover: Leet Water, The Hirsel estate

Cover design and photograph by the author

To the people of Whitsome, Swinton and Coldstream

Past, Present and Future

The Leet Water in spate, showing a surprisingly silky, smooth surface.

CONTENTS

ILLUSTRATIONS & ACCESS

The illustrations are too numerous to be listed in a separate table and they just appear within the text with unnumbered, explanatory captions, or as 'thumbnails' with explanation in the surrounding text. Most photographs are from the author's collection, and other illustrations and maps are from the stated sources.

The author stresses that he has complied with Scotland's outdoor access code stemming from the Land Reform (Scotland) Act 2003. For any readers who may follow in his footsteps, these statutory rights and obligations are summarised below:-

Access rights apply

* To all land and inland waters, unless excluded (as below);

* Access rights are for outdoor recreation, for crossing land and water, and for some educational and commercial purposes;

* Exercising access rights, and managing access land, must be done responsibly;

Where access rights do not apply

* Houses and gardens, and non-residential buildings and associated land;

* Farm buildings and yards;

* Land in which crops have been sown or are growing (although please note that the headrigs, endrigs and other margins of fields

where crops are growing are not defined as crops, whether sown or unsown, and are therefore within access rights);

* Land next to a school and used by the school;

* Sports or playing fields when these are in use and where the exercise of access rights would interfere with such use;

* Land developed and in use for recreation and where the exercise of access rights would interfere with such use;

* Golf courses (but you can cross a golf course provided you don't interfere with any games of golf);

* Places like airfields, railways, telecommunication sites, military bases and installations, working quarries and construction sites;

* Visitor attractions or other places which charge for entry.

Where it has been necessary for the author to go through e.g. farmyards to reach the Leet Water, the owners have granted permission. Also, as a matter of courtesy and because of concerns over rural theft and damage, it is good practice to contact farmers/estate owners before venturing on to any land where there are no recognised footpaths or where it is intended to walk around the margins (the headrigs and endrigs) of fields in crop.

Erratum: p. 92, caption to photograph—The stone near the well is not the stone marking St. Margaret's Walk. That stone is to the south-east of The Mount (see p. 91).

FOREWORD

by Major-General Sir John Swinton, KCVO, OBE

Ask any citizen of Berwickshire which rivers run through the County and they will almost certainly reply: Tweed, Whiteadder and Blackadder. This admirable little book will remind them that there is a fourth—the Leet—which does a valuable job of draining the prime agricultural land of the Merse.

I have a personal interest here as, although I live on the Blackadder, my ancestors acquired land astride the Leet from Eadgar, King of Scots in 1098 and, until the estate was sold out of the family in 1996, it had been in our hands for almost nine hundred years. Once surnames became fashionable, we took ours from the village of Swinton, but might so easily have called ourselves Leetwater instead!

Apart from tracing the course of the Leet from source to Tweed, this book contains a wealth of fascinating historical, archaeological and botanical detail that is a joy to read and must provide the most 'well-informed' with interesting facts they did not know. It deserves an honoured place on the bookshelves of anyone who loves Berwickshire.

The fact that the author is most generously giving all the proceeds to the Coldstream Community Centre and other groups in Whitsome and Swinton is an added reason for buying this excellent book.

John Swinton

INTRODUCTION

This book completes a trilogy of Coldstream subjects, although this is not really an accurate description because it goes further afield than the previous books, into the parishes of Whitsome and Swinton. Not very far, because the source of the Leet Water is only twelve to thirteen miles away and the last stretch of the Water comes home to Coldstream and runs alongside the built up area of the town before entering the Tweed at Tweed Green.

When I was a small boy, during and just after the Second World War, my father (initially when on leave), mother and I, with my grandmothers, aunts, uncles and cousins (not all at the same time!) often holidayed in a wooden chalet and then in a stone cottage at Llanaber in North Wales, at that time an unspoilt and idyllic place not far from Barmouth. A bubbling stream ran past the cottage and fell steeply down to the sea and the perfect sandy beaches of Cardigan Bay. Of course, the sun always shone and the bright images of the sparkling water have remained with me ever since—also, the little footpath next to it and strongly remembered smells of fruit-laden bramble bushes and waving bracken fronds that bordered its banks.

These early evocative memories are joined by those of other watery childhood adventures—making dams, fishing for sticklebacks and minnows, catching leeches and frogspawn in jam jars and then, in the Scouts, hike camping up the River Wye from Chepstow to Hereford and beside foaming torrents in Snowdonia. Later, as an adult, when living and working in Aberdeenshire, daytime and overnight mountaineering expeditions with the Cairngorm Club brought close contact (sometimes uncomfortably so) when crossing rivers and burns in Scotland. There was also masochistic, 'wild swimming' in burns and lochans that were freezing, even in summer.

Most people like rivers and the features associated with them such as waterfalls, rapids, pools—banks with sheer, sloping or gravelly sides—overhanging trees—and the secret places that are only discovered by chance. Then there are the animals, birds and insects that can be seen and the wide variety of plants that grow beside and in the water.

The major rivers of Scotland might seem to have the most obvious appeal and there are no more magnificent rivers to be seen in the British Isles than the Spey, the Dee, the Tay, the Tweed, the Clyde and the Forth. The Don, the Nith, the Findhorn, the Deveron and the Annan make up the list of the eleven major rivers of Scotland. The Tay is the longest (but not in the UK-this is the Severn) at 117 miles and has the largest catchment area in Scotland at around 2,000 square miles. Because this book is Berwickshire related, I should mention that the Tweed is the fourth longest Scottish river at 97 miles and has the second largest catchment area at about 1,500 square miles.

But, a large scale is not everything; small rivers, tributaries, mountain burns or the upper reaches of major rivers attract in other ways. They have an intimate appeal and the smaller, noisier, faster rills and burns have a special attraction with visions of sunlit picnics beside still or swirling pools and of swimming below tumbling waterfalls. Even at low level, the lazy flow of a small river or 'water', meandering through pastures and meadows has an appeal all of its own—it must do because the Leet Water usually falls into this last category and it has certainly exercised its charms on me. But, although the Leet is generally slow and placid, heavy rains and melting snow can transform its flow into a surging torrent making the fords impassable and causing short term flooding across its flood plain. This is a quite frequent occurrence.

This book, like its predecessors, is aimed at the 'potterer'—the notebook carrier with camera who records anything of interest that has individual appeal. Its chapters deal with the various sections of the Leet Water and describe things to look out for between its source in the parish of Whitsome, down through the parishes of Swinton and Coldstream to the junction with the Tweed. It does not set out to be a comprehensive history of the parishes or a guide to flora and fauna—things only crop up on an 'as and when' basis at the whim of the author during his journey down the Leet. More information on selected topics can be found in learned sources from the eighteenth century onwards, some of which are listed as further reading on page 173.

The subject matter is therefore unashamedly selective but, hopefully, it will encourage readers to find out more on topics that interest them. Readers may take an active interest by visiting the places mentioned, sometimes struggling though the undergrowth collecting nettle rash and thorns, or they may take an 'armchair' approach by following the journey on the OS Explorer maps 346 and 339—or perhaps a bit of both.

Antony Chessell, Coldstream, Scottish Borders, 2012

ACKNOWLEDGEMENTS

I wish to thank Major-General Sir John Swinton, KCVO, OBE, of Kimmerghame, for kindly agreeing to write the Foreword.

I am grateful for help, information and permissions from:-

Mr. & Mrs. R. Barclay, Leetside Farm, Duns

Michael Braithwaite, Botanical Society of the British Isles

Emily-Ieva Chessell, Melbourne, Australia

Mr. & Mrs. H. Dickson, Castlelaw Farm, Coldstream

Philip Dixon, West Newton Farm, Whitsome, Duns

Lady Caroline Douglas-Home, MBE

Ivor & Robert Gaston, Ravelaw Farm, Duns

Alistair Hodge, East Newton Farm, Whitsome, Duns

Dorothy Jenkins, Coldstream

Stephanie Metze, National Records of Scotland

Angus Miller, National Museums Scotland

Laragh Quinney, National Library of Scotland

Andrew Tulloch, Scottish Borders Libraries and Museums Service

Frank Turnbull, Coldstream & District Angling Association

Nick Yonge, River Tweed Commission

In addition, I wish to thank the Earl of Home and everyone at The Hirsel estate where the Country Park provides such a welcoming leisure facility for the people of the Borders and beyond.

Also, a special thank you to my wife, Gwen, who has accompanied me on some expeditions, put up with my absences on others and encouraged me throughout.

1

Setting the Scene

The Leet Water is something over twelve miles in length—in 1885, Francis H. Groome, editor of the *Ordnance Gazetteer of Scotland: A Survey of Scottish Topography etc.* was very specific:

> Leet Water, a rivulet of Merse district, Berwickshire, rising at a spot 1 mile NNE of Whitsome church, and 230 feet above sea-level, and flowing $13^5/_8$ miles south-south-westward and south-eastward through or along the boundaries of Whitsome, Swinton, Eccles, and Coldstream parishes, till, after a descent of 140 feet, it falls into the Tweed, $^1/_2$ mile S of Coldstream town…It has a slow and sluggish current…[1]

The *Gazetteer* may well have stated the correct figure but this must depend upon the accuracy of measurement of all the twists and turns of the Leet that are the result of its normally 'slow and sluggish current' due to the comparatively small height difference between source and mouth. This low fall means that there could be a flood risk along the course of the Leet in times of spate and the Scottish Environment Protection Agency's map showing areas with a 0.5% or greater probability of flooding in any given year, confirms this.[2] Generally, the flood plain is very much narrower in the lower reaches where the Leet is more confined, whereas in the higher reaches to the north of Swintonmill and Swinton, the wider topography means that embankments are necessary to contain the flooding. Reassuringly, the risk is not too great for most houses and farm buildings in modern times, although a few are not immune in exceptional circumstances.

The derivation of 'Leet Water' may be from the Old English *wætergelæt* meaning an open watercourse to conduct water. The Old Northumbrian dialect gives *let* and Middle Scots (the Anglic language of Lowland Scotland used until the late 16th C.) gives *leit*. So, 'Leitholm' may have derived from the Old English *gelætham* meaning a farm by the water conduit.[3] 'Leet Water' could have got its name from man-made leets, leats or lades extracting channelled water for the mills along its course such as the long gone mills north of Coldstream on The Hirsel estate. However, it is probable that the name precedes these and is more likely to have been derived from the general term for a natural watercourse.

So far, there has been no mention of the Leet as a river and there is good reason for this. A sketch map of St. Mary's Abbey, Coldstream, dated 1589 shows the Leet as the 'watter of leet'. Sharpe's map of Coldstream in 1818 describes it merely as 'Leet' and both John Blackadder's map of 1797 and Crawford and Brooke's map of 1843 show it clearly as 'Leet Water'.[4] May Williamson suggests that 'Water' is the term used in the Scottish Borders for all streams smaller than rivers and larger than burns.[5] She states that 'stream' is a rare term in Scotland and few examples are to be found in Northumberland. Even in the rest of England, it is rare as a name ending. Nevertheless, 'Coldstream' is a Scottish example and May

Williamson believes that the name might originally have been applied to the Leet Water or some other local watercourse and then been transferred to the settlement beside it.[6]

The Leet Water is often missed off any list of tributaries of the River Tweed because of its undemonstrative size. Other tributaries include the Whiteadder, the Till, the Eden, the Teviot, the Leader, the Gala, the Ettrick, the Leithen, the Quair, the Eddlestone, the Manor, the Lyne and the Holms. However, most of those (exceptions are the Till [which is mostly in England] and the Teviot) are usually named 'Water' rather than 'River' so, in Lowland Scots terminology, they are distinguishable from the major rivers.

The Leet is very unusual in terms of its directional flow in that at no point does it run in the same seaward direction as the River Tweed. Instead, it takes an opposite, up-river direction, flowing south-west from its source as far as Swintonmill before swinging south-south west and eventually south-east to meet the Tweed, but still longitudinally some $1^{1}/_{4}$ miles west of its source in Whitsome parish. This is unlike most tributaries; for example, on the lower Tweed, the River Teviot, the Eden Water and the Whiteadder Water join the River Tweed having conventionally flowed in a seaward direction. The unusual course of the Leet Water may have been determined partly by the underlying geology of the south-eastern part of the Southern Uplands of Scotland but, perhaps more importantly, by the more recent effects of glacial movement and surface deposits and scouring at the end of the last Ice Age.

A major part of the Southern Uplands of Scotland is formed of Ordovician and Silurian rocks—sedimentary rocks (see map, p. 5) that were once sands and muds laid down on the floor of the Iapetus Ocean that separated vast continents. Between 490 and 420 million years ago, the ocean closed and the continents collided in a series of collisions that eventually led to the foundation of Scotland in a final geological stage known as the Caledonian Orogeny. Also in the collisions, Scotland and England were joined together and, in the process, sediments that had formed on the bed of the ocean were heaved upwards and later compressed to form greywacke (coarse, hard, dark sandstone) and shales (finer-grained sedimentary rock composed of mud with clay minerals). In southern Scotland, there are two fault lines, the Southern Upland fault that marks the boundary with the Midland Valley to the north and the Iapetus Suture which marks the line of closure of the Iapetus Ocean.

Rocks in southern Scotland mostly originate from the Silurian, Devonian and Carboniferous periods—say from 450 to 300 million years ago but with some from preceding and succeeding periods. In the later Carboniferous period, very high oxygen levels combined with a warm climate encouraged lush plant growth that quickly grew and died to form compressed, sedimentary layers of rock including coal. Gradually, over 60 million years, the temperature dropped and an Ice Age ensued during the early Permian period. Red desert deposits also formed about 250 million years ago during the Permian period. The sedimentary rocks are interspersed with areas of eruptive igneous rocks formed from solidified volcanic lava or magma pushed up through rock faults during the Devonian and Carboniferous periods, as delineated on the geological map. In Berwickshire, the sedimentary rocks include sandstones of varying

SETTING THE SCENE

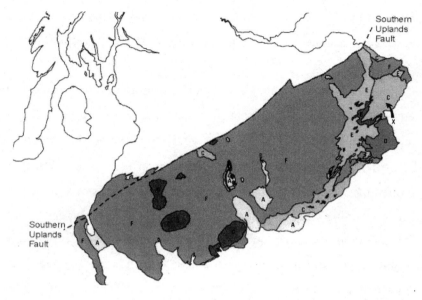

A: Permian & Triassic sedimentary rocks—299 to 200 million years ago

B: Carboniferous igneous rocks (intrusive & extrusive)—359 to 299 million years ago

C: Carboniferous sedimentary rocks—359 to 299 million years ago

D: Devonian igneous rocks (extrusive)—416 to 359 million years ago

E: Devonian sedimentary rocks—416 to 359 million years ago

F: Ordovician & Silurian sedimentary rocks—488 to 416 million years ago

G: Caledonian (Ordovician to Devonian igneous rocks (intrusive)—488 to 359 million years ago

Map reproduced by permission of National Museums Scotland and British Geological Survey.

colours from pale white to yellow or yellow-grey that have proved to be good building material for traditional houses in the area.[7] Further east, red sandstone is to be found used, for example, in the building of Ayton Castle.

The course of the Leet Water lies entirely within one of the areas of Carboniferous sedimentary rocks marked C and indicated by an arrow and cross ↖X in the top right hand corner of the geological map of the Southern Uplands of Scotland on p. 5. These rocks are termed the 'cement-stone group' because of thin bands of argillaceous (i.e. containing a substantial proportion of clay) limestone or cement-stone. The argillaceous limestone is often referred to as 'marl'.[8] The reason for the unusual course of the Leet Water is probably due to the accentuated subglacial landforms of the River Tweed valley particularly to the east of Jedburgh and Kelso. Probably towards the end of the last Ice Age, which ended about 10,000 years ago, the Tweed valley was subject to a glacial Palaeo-Ice Stream (Palaeo from Greek *palaios* meaning ancient). The ice moved downstream caused by sub-glacial melting at ground level due to the pressure of the ice above. The width of the ice-stream was constricted by the Lammermuir hills to the north and the Cheviot Hills to the south where the ice remained static. The ice-stream narrowed from its 'onset zone' width of about 24 miles south-west of Galashiels to about 12 miles in its 'trunk' from Kelso and Coldstream, eastwards.

The movement of the ice-stream caused a change in the land surface beneath the ice. Scouring of the sedimentary Carboniferous sandstones and/or deposition of material in the direction of the ice flow produced many parallel landforms of different sizes, known as 'drumlins' (from Gaelic, *druim* meaning ridge or mound). The height and width of drumlins is greater at the head (the stoss end) and tails off (the lee end) in the direction of the ice flow, as shown below. Drumlins may be 100 to 200 feet high and perhaps up to a mile or so in length and always wider than they are high, but there is great variation depending upon the rate of glacier flow and the type of deposited material.

Ice flow ➔

Section through (top) and plan of (below), a drumlin.

The Tweed valley has hundreds if not thousands of drumlins and, because all of them lie parallel to the River Tweed, it suggests that they were all laid down by only one ice-stream flowing in the one direction from west to east (or south-west to north-east) within the boundaries of the Tweed valley.[9] The effect of drumlins on the present day landscape is highly visible, for example, on the undulating road between Coldstream and Greenlaw and, very dramatically, on the 'switchback' Duns Road running north from Coldstream. The direction of flow of the Leet Water from its source near Whitsome village would therefore have been affected by the existence of the parallel drumlins that blocked any flow south-eastwards towards the Tweed. A glance at the contours on the Ordnance Survey map (Explorer 346) shows this quite clearly; the fledgling Leet had to find its way south-west instead of south-east and wind its way through lower ground around and between the drumlins before eventually turning south.

The 'switchback' Duns Road north of Coldstream has to traverse many drumlins of different heights and widths.

The present soils of Berwickshire have been formed from the rock formations mentioned earlier, by glacial action, by erosion by rain and wind, the carving out of river valleys, the decay of vegetation and by farming practices. The soils vary throughout the county and are often mixed because of different rates of erosion, and the variation in the transport and deposition of material by the Tweed and its tributaries, such as the Whiteadder Water (and the Whiteadder's own fairly large tributary, the Blackadder Water) and even by the smaller tributaries of the Tweed such as the Leet Water and its tributaries, the Harcarse and Lambden Burns.

Over the centuries, these rivers and watercourses have carved out valleys and have carried stones, gravel, sand and mud downstream in meandering channels between the drumlins and other geographical features. Periodic flooding causes overflow of the banks and the deposition of loose soil and sediments across the valley bottom known as alluvium (from the Latin *alluvius* from *alluere* meaning to wash against). The resulting alluvial plains are flat strips along the valley bottom known as haughs (perhaps deriving from *hawch* or *hawgh* in Scots or Middle English) in Scotland and the north of England. The plains are bounded by natural embankments formed when heavier boulders and gravels were left there by the floods.

The soils along the valleys and particularly the haughs comprise a rich loam sometimes above a layer of stiff clay or sometimes above gravel. Set back from the rivers are other soils of sand, clay and gravels including a light gravel, historically known as turnip soil from the ability to remove turnips from it more easily in winter compared with clay soils. There were also areas of the argillaceous limestone clays mentioned earlier. These marls, comprising clay and calcium carbonate (the latter sometimes originating from shells, giving rise to the term shell marls as opposed to clay marls) were often used in the past in Berwickshire and elsewhere as soil conditioners or fertilizers before being replaced by lime. The soils of much of Berwickshire, certainly within the parishes of Whitsome, Swinton and Coldstream, are generally very fertile and

this was recognized in 18th and 19th century accounts such as the *'Old'*
Statistical Account of Scotland, 1791-1799 and the *'New' Statistical*
Account of Scotland, 1834-1845, that described the geology and soils
within these parishes in some detail.[10]

The Leet Water runs through this fertile landscape known as
the Merse, an area extending from the Lammermuir Hills in the north,
to the River Tweed in the south with a breadth from west to east of
about twenty miles. Blaeu's *Atlas of Scotland*, 1654 describes the
Merse (in Latin) as:

> Marcia is the name of the land which first occurs on the
> boundaries of Scotland and England on the east side. For
> March means boundary, and although the vernacular
> pronunciation of the region is now Merse, the earldom of
> March, which is widely spread in this province, formerly the
> patrimony of the Dunbars, still keeps the old name.[11]

Blaeu goes on to describe the boundaries of the Merse, its history and
the character of the land and its people, including:

> ...The whole of the Merse, within the Lammermuir Hills
> which are blessed with pastures, nourishes with its fertile soil
> numerous inhabitants, in peace industrious, in war stout-
> hearted, who used to defend their possessions most bravely
> against the English...

The Merse was not entirely 'blessed' before drainage was carried out
to marshland and bog from about 1700 onwards. However, by 1813,
the Rev. James Thomson, minister of Eccles was saying that:

> ...one of the first improvements to which a judicious farmer
> [in Berwickshire, particularly the Merse] directs his attention

is draining. This is considered as one of the most important, indeed the foundation of all other improvements; for while a field is soaked in water it is of very little use. The drains which are most common are intended for carrying off the water that lodges on the surface. Every hollow in a field, which is a natural receptacle for rain, is carefully drained. Drains are usually made three feet deep, where there is a sufficient declivity to carry off the water. Some are made four, and even five feet deep...In all cases stones are preferred for filling drains: but...field stones are become scarce. In this case old thorn hedges are cut...the stems of these are into lengths...these lengths are then put into the drain, not quite vertically, but leaning upon one another...[12]

The derivation of Merse may relate to the Border areas known as Marches or it could signify the original marshy lands. It may just refer to the good arable and pasture between the Lammermuirs and the Tweed.

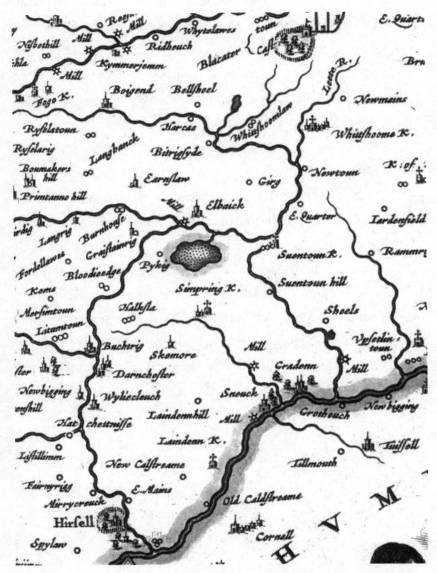

From the Blaeu *Atlas of Scotland*, 1654, showing part of 'Mercia - Berwickshire'.[13] The source of the Leet Water is near the top right corner and The Hirsel is in the bottom left hand corner. A large loch (drained in about 1700) at Swinton is almost in the centre. Reproduced by permission of the Trustees of the National Library of Scotland.

2

Source to Ravelaw

The Leet Water rises in a small copse of mixed deciduous woodland including hawthorn, ash, sycamore and other species on the eastern boundary of the present Leetside Farm in the parish of Whitsome, at OS Grid Reference NT86595180. In late spring, the area is already overgrown with nettles, as I found to my cost.

On the far side of the copse is a field still known as Leethead, but outwith Leetside farm. The field not only takes its name from the source of the Leet Water but is also a survival of the farm of that name that no longer exists. From the western edge of the present Leethead field, the Leet Water is immediately visible (but only if you know that it is there, hidden within the copse) and runs through the copse in a clearly defined channel. At the western edge of the copse, the open channel disappears beneath the arable field seen in the photograph on p. 15. At some time in the past, the watercourse was piped in order to leave a large field for efficient cropping.

Because the source is in a rather secretive place and the route westwards from the copse is underground, it might be thought that one of the other obvious watercourses shown on the Ordnance Survey map (see p.14) and seen on the ground was the real source. However, these channels are often dry for much of the year and include drainage channels along field boundaries. The spring at Leethead produces free-running water and is the true source. The Leet Water reappears at the western edge of the dotted line on the map below and at the western edge of the arable field in the photograph on p. 15.

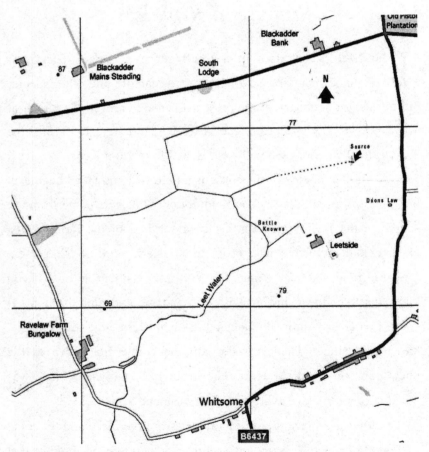

Map showing the Leet Water from its source to beyond Ravelaw Farm—the underground pipe below the first field is shown by dotted line. Each grid is 1 sq. km. Contains Ordnance Survey data © Crown copyright and database right 2012.

Looking east towards the copse containing the source of the Leet Water.

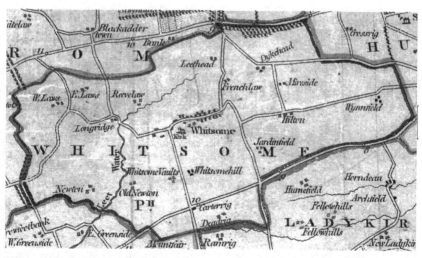

Extract from John Blackadder's map of 1797 showing Whitsome parish; the farm buildings of Leethead Farm and other farms had gone by 1834. Reproduced by permission of the Trustees of the National Library of Scotland.

It can be seen from John Blackadder's map, above, that only the Leethead farm buildings are shown in 1797.[1] The *'Old' Statistical Account of Scotland, 1791-1799*, describes Leethead as 'consisting of 44 acres, most of it good fertile ground, well worth L. 1 Sterling per acre'.[2] Leetside farm is not shown, nor does it appear on the two maps of 1820-1 by John Thomson and John Ainslie or on the map of 1826 by T. Sharp, C. Greenwood and W. Fowler.[3] However, in 1834, the Rev. Landels describes how Whitsome used to be when 'the range of land on the north side of the village was divided into several small portions, still denominated "lands". These had been owned or occupied by "portioners" but ten of them had become the southern part of Ravelaw Farm and that '"the nine" and "the eight" lay east from the preceding, and are included in the farm of Leetside'.[4] The Rev. Landels also notes that, since the time of the *'Old' Statistical Account 1791-1799*, houses and cottages on the farms of Deadrigg, Cartrigg, Myreside and Leethead had been demolished 'the first and second being annexed to Whitsome-hill, the third to Dykegatehead, and the fourth to Blackadder Bank'.[5] Frenchlaw went during the 19th century; earlier, in the 1791-99 *'Old' Statistical Account*, the Rev. George Cupples relates that it had recently become part of Mr. Boswell's estate (Blackadder Bank) and conjectures that it 'got its name from the French, either as allies or foes, having made a neighbouring eminence their station while in this part of the country'.[6]

May Williamson suggests that the name Whitsome may derive from the Middle English, *hwite husum* which could come from Old Northumberland, *hwīta hūsum* meaning, at the white houses.[7] However, Lesley Robertson refers to the possibility of a derivation from the white habits of Cistercian monks who had a settlement in the area. She also refers to a more likely explanation given in the *'New' Statistical Account*; this suggests that Whitsome comes from White or *Huite* and *Ham* or *Home*.[8] Huite was one of the witnesses to King Eadgar's charter of Coldingham, granting Swinton to the monks of St. Cuthbert sometime between 1097 and 1107 but when the charter was confirmed in 1392, the chancery clerk of Robert III wrote *Qhuite* for *Huite*. The Account states that circumstantial evidence suggests that the designation is due to 'the *residence of White*'.[9]

From the point of reappearance of the underground Leet Water, it continues in a straight line along the side of a field in a recently cleared out channel that must also have been straightened in the past. It is along this stretch that varied vegetation appears on the banks such as rosebay willowherb, docks, grasses and buttercups and low height trees such as hawthorn and cherry. Rosebay willowherb, *Epilobium angustifolium* or *Chamerion angustifolium*, was introduced from North America and was a rare plant in the 18th century. It is now well established here, having spread by seed and by underground rhizomes. A common name for it is fireweed because it thrives on land that has been consumed by fire such as bomb-sites during the Second World War. It is very invasive and has rapidly spread throughout Britain becoming rather a nuisance, despite its attractive pink flowers and fluffy seed heads. It thrives in waste ground and in wet areas and can be seen in many places along the Leet (e.g. on the channel margins on p.19), where it can cause blockages.

Another plant that I spotted at the end of this first open stretch of the Leet was sweet cicely, *Myrrhis odorata*, the liquorice plant. It

The first open straight section of the Leet Water looking south-west, beyond the culvert, showing recent clearance of the channel bed.

is quite common in Scotland although it is probably an introduced plant from a long time ago. All parts of it smell of aniseed and Richard Mabey relates that John Gerard, the 16th century herbalist used to boil the roots as a vegetable. The leaves used to be added to stewed fruit such as rhubarb, as a sweetener and even for polishing wood panels in Westmoreland. Evidently the seeds are still used as a nibble and as a salad ingredient and the oily seed cases have been used for polishing wood turning pieces.[10]

After the straight section, the Leet changes to a meandering course but, as will be described in more detail later on, the whole of the natural course of the Leet Water, from source to mouth, has been cleared and parts straightened from time to time during recent centuries. This does not mean that its course has altered substantially,

18

merely that it has been kept clear along its length with some estate works being carried out at certain points for practical reasons. In these early stretches, there are only small trees along the banks, either as single specimens, or closely planted as with some hawthorns along the first meandering stretch that have almost formed a solid hedge.

The junction of the straight and meandering stretch is also the point where water enters from drainage channels that originate as far west as Joshua Plantation (shaded grey on the map on p. 14). Thereafter, the Leet Water continues past the 'hedge' and round the side of a field shown in the photograph on p. 20, within which is a feature marked 'Battle Knowes' on the map.

Nothing remains to be seen above ground but The Royal Commission on the Ancient and Historical Monuments of Scotland (RCAHMS) has it listed as an 'Earthwork, Moated Site (Possible)' at Grid Ref. NT86125139.[11] In the *'New' Statistical Account 1834-45*, the Rev. Landels describes, 'in a field still known by the name of *Battleknowes* on the farm of Leetside, there are discernible the outlines of a camp. The form is square, and each side measures 42 yards.'[12] He conjectured that, because it was in the middle of a marsh, it would have been surrounded by water and very difficult to access and he noted that the entrance or gateway was on the south-east side, approached by a raised pavement of rough stones which had recently been dug up and removed. He believed it to have been Roman as evidenced by a copper kettle that was found by some workmen in 1827, when draining some springs nearby.[13]

However, RCAHMS do not consider the feature to be Roman, describing it, in 1954, as a circular 'fort' with diameters of 120ft. and

Battle Knowes is within the field of sheep in the middle distance with the Leet Water in the foreground. Any visible traces have now disappeared. The source copse and field boundary can still be seen on the skyline.

135ft. the site of which, when visited by the Ordnance Survey in 1956, was only 'suggested by a vague platform of smoother grass' in a pasture field. RAF aerial photographs had suggested that it was 'lozenge-shaped, with rounded corners'. In 1972, the Ordnance Survey decided that the earthwork was unsurveyable but identified 'a vague and indistinct ditch on the east and south sides' and suggested that this might have been a homestead moat. In 1979, RCAHMS confirmed it as a possible moated site with a very difficult access.[14]

Battle Knowes is not the only evidence of early human activity within the vicinity of the Leet Water. Quite close to the source is a very obvious feature known as Doons Law (Law is Scots for a rounded hill), an oval mound in the field south of Leethead field which may be a burial mound or just a glacial mound. It is planted with trees, including some dead elms and at some time has had a retaining wall built around it. RCAHMS give the dimensions as 83 ft. NE to SW and 65 ft. transversely, at Grid Ref. NT86845155 and give credence to the mound being an unexcavated and badly mutilated barrow.[15] Its origin may be uncertain but its survival would suggest that it has always had a special historical significance for local people.

Doons Law, seen from the south-east, is a prominent landmark in the field, just a few hundred yards from the source of the Leet Water.

In January 1995, ploughing turned up a cist burial, only three metres to the north of Doons Law that led to an excavation by the

Centre for Field Archaeology of Edinburgh University. The 1.05m. by 0.5m. cist comprised four upright sandstone slabs surmounted by a capstone and contained a probable female adult skeleton lying in a foetal position. There were also a decorated Northern British/Northern Rhine Beaker, four flint artefacts, a fragmented copper awl (which would have been a small, pointed tool for making holes, such as in a leather belt) and fragments of burnt bone and charcoal. Around the skeleton was an area of organic staining containing pollen grains of some type of brassica (a cabbage-like plant), alder, several ferns and meadowsweet, *Filipendula ulmaria*, the presence of the latter suggesting that it was used as a pillow or was included in a libation of some form of mead. Excavation and analysis dated the burial to the Early Bronze Age, somewhere between 2200 and 1800 BC; all the artefacts were declared Treasure Trove and allocated to the Borders Museums Service.[16]

This was not the only cist burial to have been discovered in the area. Clarke and others describe the discovery in 1831 of a cist containing bones on the south side of Doons Law. In 1839, several other cists containing bones and pottery were discovered near the mound and two others were found in 1869 and 1870. Further away, cists were found over half a mile west of Doons Law containing crouched burials accompanied by probable food vessels. About $2\frac{1}{2}$ miles to the north, near Allanton, a cist containing fragments of bone and a beaker was recorded in 1912.[17]

Within Whitsome parish, there are other springs in addition to the one that supplies the source of the Leet Water and three of these have been recorded for historical reasons. The *'New' Statistical*

Decorated Bronze Age Northern British/North Rhine Beaker c. 2200-1800 BC from the cist burial near Doons Law, Whitsome, Berwickshire. Photographed whilst on exhibition in Coldstream with permission of Scottish Borders Libraries and Museums Service.

Account records that, in 1834, two of the springs were to be found on the two vestiges of common land shared by the villagers, one to the east of the village and one on the north side, near the centre. The lands were used for bleaching, taking water from wells that were fed from the springs. The well on the east side was called The Blind Well

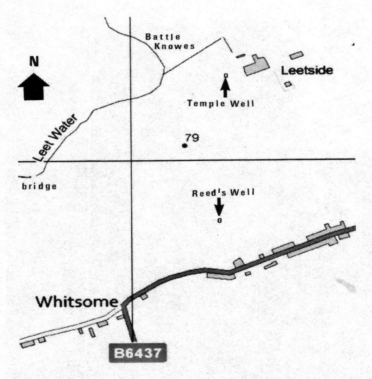

Temple Well and Reed's Well, Whitsome, superimposed on a modern map. Blind Well was east of the village in a triangular wood still shown on OS Explorer map 346. No. 79 is a spot height of 79 m. Contains Ordnance Survey data © Crown copyright and database right 2012.

because of some accident involving a blind man; the second was called Reed's Well because of a man called Reed who died near the spot following a scuffle which took place at a fair. It was said that, as a result, the villagers were deprived of the privilege of holding future fairs—a restriction that has obviously been overcome in modern times by the holding of the annual Village Fair on the first Saturday in June.[18] Reid's (Reed's) Well, is shown on the modern OS Explorer map 346. Blind Well is not on current maps, but see caption, above.

In 1832, another well built round with rough, hewn stone, was found when draining land near the head of a spring on Leetside Farm. The RCAHMS has the position recorded at Grid Ref. NT863513, just to the west of the present Leetside farm buildings. It was known as the Temple Well because there used to be a row of houses nearby named Temple Hall, perhaps because of some religious structure that once stood there. However, the RCAHMS suggest that the name of the well and the houses may be derived from the Knights Templar who are said to have owned about 40 acres of the land of Myreside, now part of the Blackadder estate. The well is no longer there but the spring was probably piped in the past into the watercourse that is shown on the modern OS map, running north-west from the Leetside farm buildings and then south-west along the side of Battle Knowes.[19]

After Battle Knowes, the Leet Water continues alongside arable field boundaries on Ravelaw Farm, at one point passing under a small bridge spanning a farm track at Grid Ref. NT85445090 and, soon after, being joined by a drainage channel just south of the farm buildings before passing under the first road bridge to be encountered on its journey to the Tweed, at Grid Ref. NT85195043. Throughout its wandering course across Ravelaw Farm, the Leet Water is narrow, sometimes with deep embankments on either side and sometimes with an open aspect across the fields, in all directions.

Sometimes there are only occasional low trees on its banks but, in other places, the banks are overgrown with small, multi-stemmed, coppiced or pollarded trees. It was a warm sunny day in early summer when I walked there and the vegetation was lush along the banks with broad-bladed grasses amongst a multitude of species of wild plants, the lack of identification of which exposed my sketchy botanical knowledge.

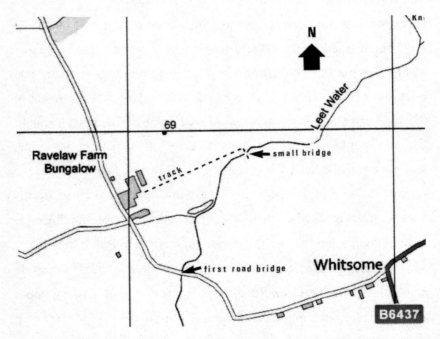

Map showing the first two bridges over the fledgling Leet Water. Each grid is 1 km. across. The no. 69 shows a spot height of 69 m. Contains Ordnance Survey data © Crown copyright and database right 2012.

The small bridge carrying the farm track (mentioned on p. 25) must be old. It might seem surprising that such a well-built bridge is to be found in this location; a modest farm track and field access (see

Small bridge taking a farm track above the Leet Water, Ravelaw Farm.

map on p. 26) might have made use of a ford. However, old maps, including John Blackadder's map of 1797, show what was probably the hamlet of Ravelaw, further to the east than the present farm buildings. The one-inch to the mile Ordnance Survey map, First Edition, 1864, Sheet 26, shows that, because of this, the track assumed a greater importance by serving as a more direct route from the hamlet (although only one small building remained by then) to the village and particularly for church-going, in preference to the public road. The through route is not shown on the Second Edition map in 1897 and there is no evidence of it on the ground today, but the well-constructed barrel arch of the bridge with its very precise voussoires topped by random rubble walls and coping stones, seems to confirm its one-time, higher status.

Ravelaw Farm does not appear on Blaeu's *Atlas of Scotland* in 1654 but it can be clearly seen as Reevelaw on John Blackadder's map. It is said that the Rev. Henry Erskine lived and preached there after he was expelled from his parish of Cornhill, Northumberland on 24th August, 1662 (St. Bartholomew's Day) following the Act of Uniformity of that year (hence the so-called Bartholomew Act) and before he became minister of Chirnside.[20] The Act of Uniformity, an English Act passed in the reign of Charles II, required all Church of England services to be conducted in accordance with the rites and ceremonies in the Book of Common Prayer and for all ministers to be ordained by recognized bishops. This was contrary to the doctrines under the Commonwealth and, as a result, nearly 2000 clergymen left the Church of England in what was known as the Great Ejection. In 1831, a memoir related that, in 1687, Henry Erskine:

> removed with his family to Rivelaw (sic), where his people erected a meeting-house. This hamlet, in common with many old villages, seems to have almost entirely disappeared: but, if we are not misinformed, there is still at least, one inhabited house that bears the name of Rivelaw.[21]

Henry Erskine inspired many others, including Thomas Boston of Ettrick (1676-1732), the Duns-born pastor and author of *Human Nature in its Fourfold State* who records that his father took him to a Presbyterian meeting in Newton of Whitsome where he heard and was much influenced by the preaching of Henry Erskine. Thereafter, he:

was set to pray in earnest. I also attended, for ordinary, the preaching of the word at Rivelaw, where Mr. Erskine had his meeting house, about four miles from Dunse.[22]

It would seem that Henry Erskine preached at Ravelaw and at Newton (in 18th C. called Old Newton, in 19th C. called Whitsome Newton, but now East Newton)—see Chapter 3. He also preached in Whitsome Church. The *'Old' Statistical Account, 1791-1799*, records that:

Ravelaw and East Laws, the property of Sir Alexander Don, Baronet, occupied in one farm, consists of 466 acres, the rent of which is L. 372. Along with some wet, marsh, low lying ground, it contains no small proportion of good, fertile, dry, and well exposed ground, well improved, and skillfully cultivated.[23]

The family seat of the Don family was Newton Don, near Stichill, the estate having been purchased by them in the 17th century. Ravelaw farm came into the family's ownership at the beginning of the 18th century, through a female line. During the 19th century, financial problems led to the sale of Ravelaw and it came into the ownership of the Marquis of Tweeddale and remained so until after the First World War.[24]

Over the centuries, Ravelaw, like most of the farms in the area, was managed by tenant-farmers and four were listed in the census returns between 1841 and 1911. In the 18th century, the Historical Tax Records show that, in 1797-8, John Roughhead was one of only five residents of Whitsome & Hilton parish to pay tax of 5s. $7^{1}/_{2}$d on one clock and one silver or metal watch; he is also listed as one of 20 tenant farmers in Whitsome and had 13 horses of which

The narrow Leet Water in its upper reaches as it crosses Ravelaw Farm, looking back towards Battle Knowes.

10 were classed as working horses, attracting duty of £1.[25] The census records for all the farms show the large number of grieves, stewards, farm workers, family members, servants and trades people who were living and working on the farms in Whitsome during the 19th century.

Ravelaw is now combined with the nearby Langrigg Farm which is shown on Blackadder's map as Longridge. In the *'Old' Statistical Account*, Langrigg is described as:

> A long narrow strip of land, consisting of 155 acres Scots measure, or 186 English. It is low, but well improved and skillfully cultivated, as it has very long been in the occupation of the proprietor, its rent cannot be precisely ascertained, but it is not over-rated in its present state at L. 1 Sterling per acre, and of course gives L. 186. It is the property of Joshua Tait, Esq; and gives a vote for a Member of Parliament. This estate pays only 6s. 8d. to the minister, the supposed conversion of a boll of oats of old; the new stipend not yet localled.[26]

The *Account* also states, 'It is extraordinary, that no one heritor or proprietor has so much as a house within the parish, except Joshua Tait Esq'. Also, the presence of a resident proprietor provides 'a degree of urbanity, politeness, and subordination, very salutary to society; industry is rewarded, ingenuity and arts flourish'[27] The status of an owner-occupied property that carried with it a parliamentary seat, is reflected in the architecture of the original farmhouse despite subsequent alterations; it has a C (S) listing from Historic Scotland. However, to be fair, Leetside, with more surviving original elements, commands a higher, B listing.[28] In 1834, the owner of Longridge was George Taitt (sic) who:

during the current season…has tried an experiment altogether new in this part of the country; on the more extensive adoption and ultimate success of which may depend important consequences both to proprietors and labouring classes. By trenching a small field, at a cost of L. 4. 10s. an acre, and then sowing it in barley, instead of leaving it fallow, as it must have been, according to the usual rotation, above an average crop of good quality was the produce.[29]

The above is an interesting reference to an improvement in farming practice that was being trialled in Britain called trenching or spade husbandry and written up in agricultural journals of the day.[30] Instead of ploughing land in the summer and letting it lie fallow before planting the following year, land was dug over by spade immediately after cropping and sown immediately with a high yielding cereal such as barley. The method was very labour intensive, but it meant that the land was not out of production for a season and it provided extra employment. The trials showed that it was worth the effort in terms of economic benefit and, in 1834, George Tait(t) must have been at the forefront of this new development in Scotland.

Langrigg farmhouse has now become Ravelaw farmhouse. South-east of Ravelaw farm buildings, the Leet Water passes under the bridge carrying the minor road between Whitsome village and the B6460 road, at Grid Ref. NT85195043. The bridge is probably very old, but repairs carried out over the years to ensure its safety for carrying traffic and, in more recent times, road traffic, have disguised any real sense of antiquity. This is not helped by the prominent tuck pointing to the stonework and the abundance of cement used for

South-west aspect of the Ravelaw road bridge with Ravelaw farmhouse (formerly Langrigg) in the distance

bedding the coping stones, all of which gives an appearance which is at odds with vernacular construction in the Borders.

I enjoyed walking along the Leet Water as far as Ravelaw. There is an open aspect to the route now with trees confined to linear routes, boundaries and copses, but it must have been quite different in prehistoric times, particularly in the Bronze Age when the people associated with the many burial cists were living there. It was probably heavily wooded with clearings for settlements and unenclosed farming; even then the Leet Water must have played its part in the daily lives of the local tribe. It is interesting to speculate.

3

Ravelaw to Swintonmill

Beyond the Ravelaw road bridge, the Leet Water continues on its shallow, winding way towards Whitsome East Newton farm. Along this stretch, the Leet Water collects water from two tributaries on the west side, the Redlaw Burn to the north of West Newton and the longer, Harcarse Burn which joins the Leet Water south of West Newton. The Harcarse Burn has its own tributary, the Blubbery Burn and both rise in Fogo parish, with the Harcarse Burn taking its name from the properties of Harcarse and Harcarse Hill. May Williamson believes that Harcarse may be Celtic in origin although there is also a Middle English derivation, *hāre-carr(es)* meaning grey rocks.[1] However, there is always difficulty in interpretation when dealing with place names—in this case, according to several on-line (Scots to English) dictionaries, *carse* refers to a stretch of land along a river bank. In addition to the two burns, there are also farm drainage ditches and channels that flow into the Leet Water, all adding to the flow of water.

The Leet Water passes through East Newton farm and West Newton farm before it leaves Whitsome parish and enters Swinton

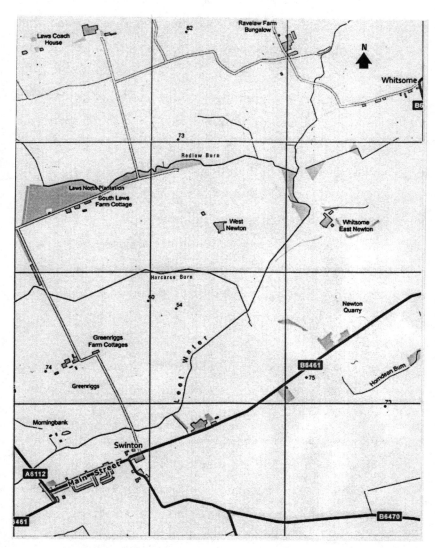

Map showing the Leet Water from Ravelaw, past East and West Newton farms to Swinton village. Each grid is 1 sq. km. Contains Ordnance Survey data © Crown copyright and database right 2012.

parish at the point of entry of the Harcarse Burn. In 1799, the *'Old'* *Statistical Account* records East Newton as being:

the property of James Dickson of Anton's Hill, Esq; consists of about 250 acres, much exceeding indeed in moisture, but containing more good, dry, and fertile land than the former (West Newton). It is rented at L. 160, upon a lease nearly expiring; and this farm, along with 17 detached acres at the north-east corner of it, rented at L. 17…constitutes the property of Mr. Dickson in this locality.[2]

In 1834, the landowner of East Newton (referred to then as Old Newton) was Robert Brown Esq.[3] There is no further mention of the whereabouts of the building that had been used as a dissidents' meeting-house in the 17th century. The principal quarry in the parish was at Old Newton and this supplied best quality freestone 'out of which the chief edifices in Berwickshire have been built'.[4]

West Newton was the property of Charles Buchan Esq. in 1799 when it:

consists of 250 acres, rented at L. 130, upon a new lease (for it has long been occupied by the present tenant and his father), which commenced at Whitsunday 1794, the validity of which is now disputed by the proprietor, in a process before the Court of Session. Seventy acres of it are bad, extremely so, being moory and marshy, from the watery situation of the farm, which renders it often inaccessible from most quarters; it is usually called Buchan's Isle.[5]

In 1834, the landowner of West Newton (referred to then as New Newton) was Robert Brown, Esq, also the owner of East Newton.[6] It is clear that, in the 18th century, there were great problems caused by marshy and waterlogged land resulting in stagnant pools, foggy air and resultant diseases. This would have been made worse by the poor standard of rural dwellings occupied by agricultural labourers and their families, whose houses would have been subject to dampness and, often, flooding. However, by 1834, steps had been taken to improve the situation by drainage and reclamation. Nevertheless:

> Some intelligent men are of opinion, that draining might be carried out to a greater extent with much advantage, if facilities were afforded by the erection of a tile and brick kiln in the neighbourhood, as it is now difficult to obtain a sufficient quantity of stones for the purpose. Little more than a quarter of a century ago, a considerable portion of the now fertile farms of Dykegatehead, Wynnefield, Leetside, and others, was overflowed. Much praise is due to the present tenants and their immediate predecessors for the skilful management and persevering zeal with which they have prosecuted the work of amelioration.[7]

It was also noted in 1834 that:

> Small bridges and conduits have been thrown over all the watercourses, which formerly crossed the public roads at numerous points, and often rendered them impassable during heavy rains, and in winter.[8]

Since then, tiled field drains and regular clearance of the Leet Water have transformed the situation. In more recent times, major widening and deepening of the whole of the Leet Water and one of its tributaries, the Lambden Burn, together with allied field drainage work in Berwickshire, was carried out in 1973 with the aid of an EU Agricultural Fund (FEOGA) grant of £31,643.[9]

Extract from John Blackadder's map of 1797 showing the Leet Water between Reevelaw (Ravelaw) and Swinton village. Compare this with the maps on pp. 35 and 39. Reproduced by permission of the Trustees of the National Library of Scotland.

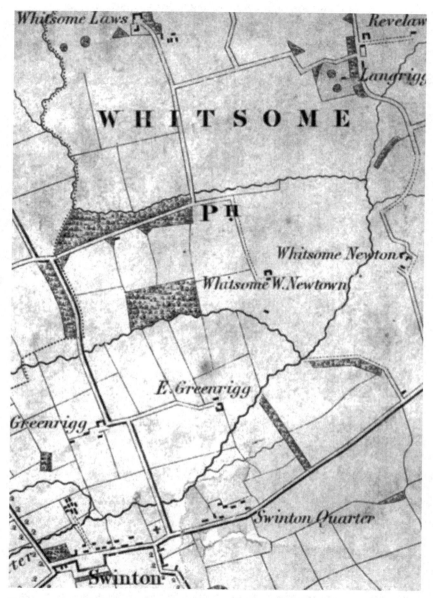

Extract from William Crawford's and William Brooke's map of 1843 showing the Leet Water between Revelaw (Ravelaw) and Swinton village. Reproduced by permission of the Trustees of the National Library of Scotland.

A comparison between Blackadder's map, Crawford and Brooke's map and the modern map on p. 35, shows some differences, mostly concerning the farms, although Crawford and Brooke's map also shows more detail in respect of field boundaries and woodland.[10] Both of the Newton farms appear with slight name changes and the farms of East Greenside and West Greenside become East and West Greenrigg in 1843. Today, West Greenrigg has become Greenriggs and East Greenrigg has disappeared altogether. Two other farms that have gone since they appeared on Blackadder's map (although they are not shown separately) are East and West Whitsome Vaults. These are intriguing names but they are explained by the Rev. Cupples in 1799:

> East and West Vaults got their names from certain Vaults, formed of old in several places of this parish, for secreting their effects, upon any alarm from the south.[11]

The underground chambers would have been much needed during the many troubles in the Scottish Borders, but the names could only have arisen long after the need for secrecy had disappeared. In 1799, the Earl of Wemyss owned the farms; at the time, the West Vaults farm was tenanted by John Hogarth and another unknown tenant occupied the East Vaults farm. Both farms contained '28 souls in 7 families'.[12] Whitsome Vaults appear on John Thomson's Atlas of 1832 but not on the Ordnance Survey Six-inch 1st edition map of the area in 1862.[13]

At the nearest point to East Newton farm, the Leet Water turns south-west, passing under a footbridge surfaced with railway sleepers and carrying a pipe across to woodland on the West Newton side at Grid Ref. NT85174946. Further south-west, the Leet Water passes under a concrete-slabbed bridge carrying a farm track (see map below). At East Newton, I was glad that I was wearing Wellington boots as I tracked along the side of a field and along the overgrown bank. It was difficult to see the running water looking towards the footbridge because of the undergrowth but, looking north-east, as the Leet Water came round the bend, the surface was more obvious. On the west bank, there are young trees shown on the map below (grey shading) that must have been planted since the last major revision of the OS Explorer map in 2000 (selected revisions only in 2005/6).

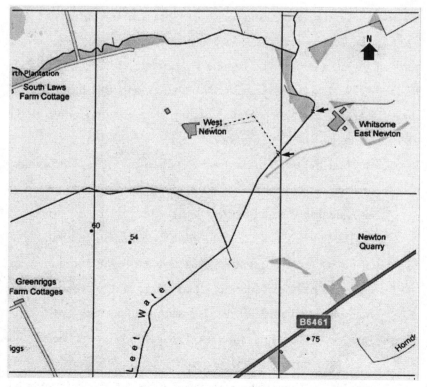

Map with arrows pointing to the footbridge at East Newton and the farm track bridge at West Newton. Each grid is 1 sq. km. Contains Ordnance Survey data © Crown copyright and database right 2012.

At West Newton farm, the landscape is more open again as the Leet Water passes under a concrete-surfaced farm track bridge that has a rather disengaged 'guard' rail along the north-east side, Grid Ref. NT84994920. This is a very straight stretch of the Leet Water on both sides of the bridge for about one third of a mile that would suggest some artificial channeling in the past, confirmed by comparing it with the Blackadder and Crawford maps. At the south-western end of this, it then bends further south on another straight stretch, again for about a third of a mile until it reaches the point of entry of the Harcarse Burn from the north-west. At this point, the Leet Water passes out of Whitsome parish and into Swinton parish.

The Leet Water, from Harcarse Burn as far as the road bridge north of Swinton church and cemetery ('cemetery bridge'), Grid Ref. NT83874779, runs between artificial embankments that have been in place for a long time, to prevent flooding across the widening flood plain. As long ago as 1799, the Rev. Cupples records that:

> Betwixt the two longitudinal elevations or ridges of Swinton quarter and Greenrigg lies a flat low piece of ground of a very considerable breadth, often overflowed by the swellings of the Leet, which great pains have been taken to drain, and which is most productive of grass, and even sometimes of corn in a very dry summer. If the large and expensive canal, made by William Hall, Esq; to secure a spacious bed for the Leet while passing through his grounds, were continued westward through Lord Swinton's lands to Swinton Mill, it would contribute much to the fertility of the soil and the health of the inhabitants.[14]

The 'cemetery bridge', looking north.

So, it seems William Hall had already done major works at that time to the east of Swinton village. This would have been William Hall of Whitehall, near Chirnside who, in about 1754, had purchased three farms from Lord Swinton and later sold them on to Lord Elibank for more than double the price.[15] The Swinton family had sold these, as well as other farms, to recoup losses resulting from their support of Cromwell during the Civil War, although they still retained a large estate.

Greenrigg(s) and Swinton Quarter referred to by the Rev. Cupples, can both be seen on the map on p. 44. Apart from its general use as a fourth part of anything, part of the stern of a ship or a military lodging, 'quarter' is a Scots term for a locality or district—in this case the long-established farm of that name. Quarter may have been a

43

quarter of a larger Scots land measure such as a davoch, which, with its third, quarter, fifth, or eighth parts, must have originated from farming practices that determined manageable areas for ploughing, sowing or harvesting and became known as oxgangs, ploughgates, penny-lands and many other terms. Definition is not helped by regional differences, whether Highland or Lowland or East or West Scotland and whether the origins were, say, Celtic, Norse, or Anglo-Saxon.[16]

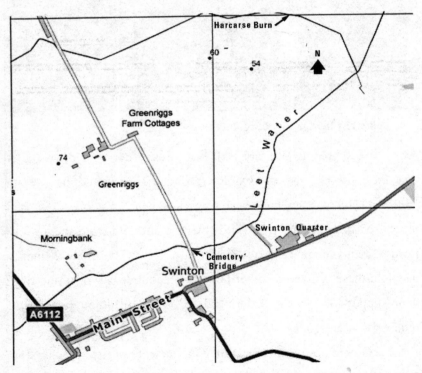

The Leet Water from the Harcarse Burn to Swinton village (north side). Each grid is 1 sq. km. Contains Ordnance Survey data © Crown copyright and database right 2012.

By 1834, drainage and channeling of the Leet had improved in Swinton because, under the heading of 'husbandry', the Rev. Logan says:

> the only improvement of any general importance which has recently been effected, is the deepening and widening of the bed of the Leet, which used to overflow its banks occasionally, to the great injury of the contiguous grounds, as, from its being almost quite level, the water became stagnant upon it in many places.[17]

Today, the containment of the Leet Water with embankments can be seen clearly to the east of the 'cemetery bridge' and, when I was there, there was a clearly defined channel. There are similar defences on the west side of the bridge, but there are overhanging trees on this side so the route does not look as open or as clear cut, but is more attractive. I climbed down below the bridge to get a better view of the attractive, sylvan setting on the southern bank as the Leet Water takes a loop and starts to make its way behind the church and the properties on the north side of Main Street, Swinton.

From below the bridge, there are several species of trees looking downstream, but one overhanging the water is a variety of willow, probably the common osier, *Salix viminalis*, although there are other varieties as well as hybrids. This and other osiers along the banks of the Leet Water will have been coppiced or pollarded in the past, in order to provide a constant source of regenerated stems from the stump. Willows respond well to coppicing, producing fast growing stems helped by the tree's preferred habitat alongside rivers and ditches and in rich soil that is subject to flooding. The stems were traditionally used for making baskets.

The 'cemetery bridge' carries the minor road north from the B6461 to Greenriggs. The road links the two ridges (both are drumlins) described by the Rev. Cupples in 1799 (see p. 42) by crossing the flood plain of the Leet Water. The single-span stone bridge, whether original or not, is still old, but its piers have been strengthened and supported by modern low buttresses at their base. The bridge parapets are in good condition but, again, the prominent tuck-pointing does not look correct.

One of the coping stones on the east parapet has a curious circular design carved into it with some lettering that is facing away from the road and is illegible due to weathering and a partial covering of lichen. Perhaps it is a reused memorial from the churchyard, or could it be an ancient sundial?

From the 'cemetery bridge', the Leet Water continues in a roughly south-westerly direction past Morningbank and passes under the road bridge which carries the A6112 road to Mount Pleasant and Duns. Past the road bridge, the Leet Water still runs between high embankments on its way to Morningbank.

The OS Six-inch 1st edition map, surveyed in 1858 shows 'Old Clay Pits' to the east and south of Morningbank and north-west of the Leet Water.[18] The clay pits would have provided the material for making bricks, tiles and drainage pipes; they are not featured on Blackadder's or Crawford's maps and they no longer exist, the only evidence that they were once there being a marshy and reeded area (in summer when I was there) with scattered potsherds that I came across, nearby.

Bridge carrying the A6112 road north from Swinton village.

Perhaps the clay was fired in a kiln at Morningbank but, if not, it could have been transported to kilns elsewhere in Berwickshire that were needed during the 19th century for farm improvements—the pipes for better land drainage, the tiles and bricks for farm buildings and the characteristic brick chimneys for the steam powered threshing machines. It is known, for example, that there was a tile works at Fallsidehill farmsteading near Hume but there would have been many others.[19]

The current map on p. 44 shows a surviving pond just south of Morningbank which is the marshy and reeded area mentioned above and which was used as the curling pond for the village, according to an OS map of 1903.[20] It still retains a definite rectangular shape from when it was used for curling. Morningbank is now a distribution centre for LPG bottled gas for home heating and, consequently, has areas where public access rights do not apply. The

47

stone bridge carrying the main A6112 road north from Swinton to Mount Pleasant, Grid Ref. NT83134749, has stone parapets with half-round coping stones and semi-circular caps to the piers giving a more vernacular appearance compared with others.

The view from the road bridge looking north-east back towards the former Morningbank clay-pits shows a straight section of the Leet Water, between embankments. I saw large clumps of yellow flag, *Iris pseudacorus*, growing in the bed of the Leet, although they were not in flower when I was there. The plant is very invasive and spreads quickly by underground rhizomes and by seed. In 1835, George Johnston, in his *The Natural History of the Eastern Borders*, describes the watery habitat of the 'Water flag: Yellow Sedge: The Segge' and quotes:

> The plant is used by coopers. The dried leaves are put between the steps of barrels to prevent leakage. Under the name of Swords they furnish youthful warriors with a weapon. On the banks of the Whiteadder and Blackadder bundles of Seggs tied together used to be employed by children learning to swim. Some of our common people identify our plant with the flags by the river's brink, in which the ark of bull-rushes containing the infant Moses was secreted. J. Hardy.[21]

South-west of the A6112 road bridge, the Leet Water flows across land that is shown in early maps as being part of the policies of Swinton House, belonging to the Swintons of Swinton. Blackadder's map of 1797 shows the Leet Water flowing through quite formal

enclosures around Swinton House. By 1843, Crawford shows the
policies but also a well-defined field pattern and an agricultural use
that has remained until the present day although many field
boundaries have been removed to create larger fields. A comparison
between the earlier maps and the modern map shows surprisingly

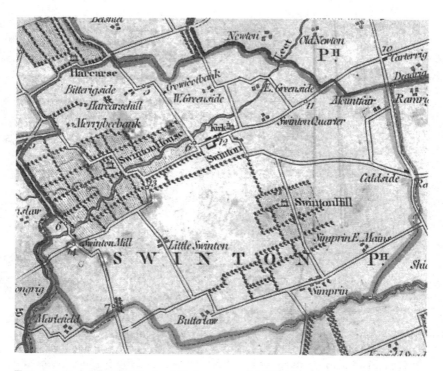

**Extract from John Blackadder's map of 1797 showing the Leet Water
flowing through Swinton parish. Reproduced by permission of the
Trustees of the National Library of Scotland.**

little change although the Leet Water now runs a much straighter
course through Swinton parish. Blackadder's map shows a blank area
west of Swinton Hill; this must have been the site of a large loch
shown on Blaeu's *Atlas of Scotland* (see p. 12) that, according to the

49

Rev. Logan in 1834, had been drained since 1700. He also refers to 'only one stream, and that inconsiderable—the Leet...'[22]

Earlier, in 1799, the Rev. Cupples had also noted that 'the only stream of any note in the parish is Leet, which abounds in pike'.[23]

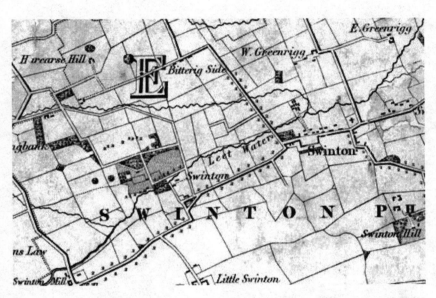

Extract from William Crawford's and William Brooke's map of 1843 showing the Leet Water flowing through Swinton parish. The ornamental policies around Swinton House have been reduced since 1797. Reproduced by permission of the Trustees of the National Library of Scotland.

The Royal Commission on the Ancient and Historical Monuments of Scotland (RCAHMS) provides a succinct entry for Swinton House (Grid Ref. NT81824706), within its Canmore archive:

Swinton House forms the core of the estate of Swinton, which for around nine centuries was in the hands of the Swinton family, who were responsible for the building of the structures which still survive here [and which are listed individually for Swinton village and estate with archaeological and historical notes in the Canmore archive].

The existing Swinton House replaced an earlier structure which burned down in 1797 [1792?]. Dated 1800, it is a two-storeyed structure built in the Neo-Classical style using ashlar masonry. There is an adjoining wing on the west side which may represent a surviving portion of the earlier structure...[24]

The derivation of the name of the village as well as the estate, arises from the very long and unbroken lineage of the Swinton family whose name, in turn, was always said to have originated from the bravery of an ancestor with Saxon roots who gained the inheritance by clearing the country of wild boar or swine. The family, which has included many distinguished titled and military figures down the centuries, has recognized this in their crest of a boar chained to a tree and the inclusion of three boars' heads in their armorial bearings. There have been other explanations for the derivation of the name, e.g., May Williamson notes that *Swein*, son of Ulfkill held Swinton in 1100, so that the first element of Swinton may be from Old Norse, *sveinn* or Middle English, *swein*, or *swain*, rather than the Old English origin, *swin*, meaning pig or boar.[25] However, the family explanation goes back a long way and I like to think that the name does derive from *swin*, meaning boar and the brave deeds of the Swinton ancestor.

The Swinton family association with the area continues today, by descent through the Kimmerghame branch of the family. Kimmerghame was built in the 1850s on the site of an earlier house that was owned in the early part of the 18th century by Sir Andrew Home, the younger brother of the 2nd Earl of Marchmont.[26] Swinton has been a combined parish with Simprin since 1761, slightly later than the combination of the parishes of Whitsome with Hilton, which came together in 1735. Both amalgamations took place for administrative reasons such as the movement away of a minister and/or convenience in terms of population numbers and distribution within the former parishes and not because of religious strife. Hilton, Simprin and the former Whitsome churches are now ruins.

Swinton village, with its cottages, village green and church, is at the heart of the parish. The present church, on the site of a former church and perhaps incorporating parts of it, dates from 1729 with subsequent improvements and extensions being carried out throughout the 18th and 19th centuries and substantial improvements designed by the Edinburgh architect, Sir Robert Lorimer in 1910. Generations of the Swinton family are buried within the church.[27]

Having passed through the fields that may once have been part of the extended policies of Swinton House as described on pp. 48-9, the Leet Water flows under a small bridge carrying the road north past the East Lodge of Swinton House. The bridge, at Grid Ref. NT82344708, has a single arch with stone parapets. On the map on p. 54, it is where the arrow points between East Lodge and Kelso Road. Trees, including hawthorn and willow, overhang the Leet Water giving a restricted view on both sides of the bridge. The road here is very straight as are many of the roads across the Merse, reflecting not only historic field and farm boundaries, but also ancient trackways laid down along direct routes, long before farm enclosures.

Small bridge over the Leet Water on the road leading past the East Lodge of Swinton House. This view looking south-east towards the junction (in the distance) with the B6461 road.

From here, the Leet Water passes to the north-west of Swinton Bridge End farm and flows through a wooded area and beneath a bridge carrying the southern access track to Swinton House at Grid Ref. NT82034688. The RCAHMS record for the bridge describes it as a single-span, hump-backed structure built in the early 19th century.[28] The record for Swinton Bridge End shows that the farmhouse was built in the early to mid-nineteenth century and is unusual in that most of its original details, including doors and windows, remain substantially unchanged. It is built of sandstone rubble with brick chimney stacks, a common feature in the Scottish Borders.[29]

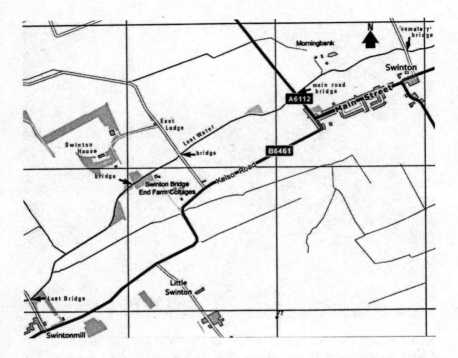

Map showing the course of the Leet Water from 'cemetery bridge' in the north-east to Leet Bridge in the south-west. 1 sq. km. grids. Contains Ordnance Survey data © Crown copyright and database right 2012.

This is an attractive old bridge and, as it does not carry a public road, its parapets have not been 'enhanced' by inappropriate pointing. The piers and parapets project in front of the arch on both bridge faces and the projecting parapets are carried on attractive stone corbelling. The piers are faced with stugged (tooled) ashlar blocks with recent angled and rectangular concrete buttresses at water level, for support. The bridge would have been a handsome feature when it was built and I wonder whether it was a survival from the time of the old house before that was burnt down.

The north-east face of the hump-back bridge showing the corbelling.

However, its building may coincide with or follow on from the rebuilding of Swinton House in 1800 by John Swinton (1759-1820), 28th of that Ilk, Advocate and Sheriff of Berwickshire from 1793 until his death. Unfortunately, the stonework has been 'patched up' with cement, infilling a number of crevices and obscuring many of the ashlar blocks. Nevertheless, the bridge retains two old circular pillars at the north-west ends of each of the parapets and is still an attractive, if rather a worn-looking structure.

The bridge is indicated by an arrow south-east of Swinton House on the map on p. 54. From here, the Leet Water flows south west, through or past small areas of woodland and then open farmland until it is crossed by the Leet Bridge, Grid Ref. NT81324608, just north-west of Swintonmill.

Leet Bridge north of Swintonmill, south-west face.

The Leet Bridge carries a minor road connecting the B6461 road at Swintonmill, north-westwards to the B6460 road, just south west of Mount Pleasant. The RCAHMS record for the bridge suggests that it may date from the late 18th century and states:

> The bridge consists of three arches. Most of the structure is built of sandstone rubble bound in mortar, but the arches are more ornate in appearance. Each of the individual stones which make up the arch, known as voussoirs, is formed from a dressed block of sandstone.[30]

The tight semi-circular shape of the three side-by-side arches springing from stone pads on the piers, is reminiscent to me of a

56

Roman bridge or an aqueduct, although on a small scale. The parapets and random rubble stonework have received much care and attention from Scottish Borders Council Roads Department, including new coping stones on the parapets and tuck pointing in cement rather than lime mortar. However, the arches and piers when viewed from water level leave no doubt that this is an old bridge. An attractive feature is the rebate to the voussoirs on the central arch and the projecting keystone in the centre.

Looking north-east from Leet bridge in the direction of the hump-back bridge (although this is over half a mile away), the banks of the Leet Water are covered in vegetation including many coppiced osiers. This restricted view is quite different from the view looking south-west from Leet Bridge (see p. 58) which is an open scene as the Leet Water flows between arable fields. To the south-east of Leet Bridge, is Swintonmill, a collection of once derelict farm buildings that is being renovated and converted into a residential development. According to RCAHMS, the farm buildings are shown on plans dating from 1803 drawn up by architects George Lawrie and William Waddell.

At that time, 'the farmsteading included a range of facilities, such as cattle courts and shelters, stables and barns. It also included a windmill, which may once have powered a threshing machine'. The windmill would have preceded the advent of steam power for threshing, with the associated tall brick chimneys above the steam engine houses that became characteristic of the farming landscape throughout Berwickshire in the 19th century.[31] There is no record of any mill powered from a lade taken from the Leet Water unlike

Leitholm Mill to the south-west which was powered from a lade taking water from the Lambden Burn.

Looking south-west from Leet Bridge, just north of Swintonmill.

RAVELAW TO SWINTONMILL

Swintonmill is the last of the farms traversed by the Leet Water before leaving Swinton and Simprin parish. Comparing modern OS maps with earlier maps, it is interesting to note that many of the farms and farm names still survive within the parish, such as Mountfair, Swinton Quarter, Harcarse, Greenriggs (Greenrigg and Greenside), Crowfootbank, Swinton Hill, Simprin Mains, Little Swinton and Butterlaw. A few have disappeared, such as the intriguingly named Bitterigside and Merrybeebank.

Earlier, mention was made of the 18th century Horse Tax surveys and the Clock and Watch Tax surveys that listed the liability of the occupants of farms in Whitsome parish. The survey records show that the occupants of Swinton and Simprin incurred similar liabilities for Horse Tax in 1797-98, ranging from one horse each for residents in Swinton village, up to twelve horses each for William Hunter at Swinton Hill, James Thomson at New Swinton and Peter Thomson at Mountfair, who each paid £1. 4s. 0d. in duty. The Rev. Cupples had two horses, both liable for duty at a total of 4s. 0d.

Whereas only five Whitsome residents were liable for Clock and Watch duty in 1797-98, ten Swinton residents were liable, with a total of twenty clocks and watches. James Thomson of New Swinton had one clock, one gold watch (the only one listed in the parish) and two silver or metal watches, for which he paid 15s. 0d,, twice as much as John Swinton, Sherriff, of Swinton House, who only paid 7s. 6d. for one clock and two silver or metal watches.[32]

At the end of Chapter 2, I mentioned my enjoyment at walking much of the first section from the source of the Leet Water as far as Ravelaw. I have also enjoyed the route from Ravelaw to

Swintonmill; my method for this section has been to walk some parts and to 'dip in and out' at other points, depending upon circumstances. The route has still been through open country but there have also been more pockets of woodland. But, as the Leet Water has grown gradually, there have been more old bridges—and they are getting larger. I haven't come into contact with prehistory to the same extent although I know that it must have been all around me—this is an old landscape. From East and West Newton onwards, the Leet Water has turned more to the south-west and even further away from the direction of flow of the River Tweed into which it will eventually discharge. A quite strange phenomenom mentioned earlier and one dictated by the geography of the Merse.

4

Swintonmill to Charterpath Bridge

From Swintonmill, the Leet Water starts to make a turn towards the south along the side of woodland that can be seen skirting the bank on the map below. At Leitholm Bridge, it is even heading south-east, but then flows south, south-east and south-west.

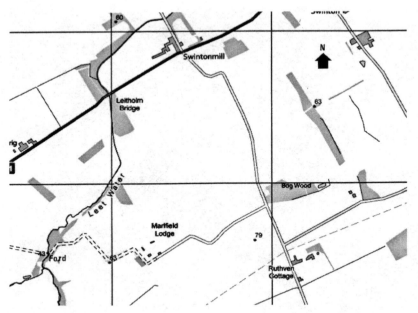

Map showing the Leet Water from Swintonmill to Marlfield. Each square is 1 sq. km. Contains Ordnance Survey data © Crown copyright and database right 2012.

The present Leitholm Bridge, at Grid Ref. NT80984557, was built in 1904; the date can be faintly seen on a plaque on the south face, over the arch. The date 1992 has also been inscribed to show the date of renovation. The bridge carries the B6461 road between Leitholm and Swinton. From the point where the Leet Water meets the trees west of Swintonmill right down to a point opposite Darnchester Mains, the Leet forms the boundary with Eccles parish to the west; Eccles parish includes the village of Leitholm. Marlfield, shown on the above map, is just within the parish of Coldstream. The rusticated regular sandstone blocks of the parapet are light yellow sandstone whereas the voussoirs of the arch and the snecked rubble blocks below the parapet are of pink sandstone.

South face of Leitholm Bridge.

SWINTONMILL TO CHARTERPATH BRIDGE

The Leet Water, although still fairly narrow and shallow at this point, is gradually increasing in size as it gathers more water from drainage channels that feed in along the whole stretch between the Harcarse Burn and Leitholm Bridge. I have heard it said that 'the Leet Water is just a drain', a rather dismissive view inferring that it is only a conduit for sewage, waste-water and agricultural chemicals. Until recently, such criticism might have had some validity and the Scottish Environment Protection Agency has stated that, in 2002, 'diffuse pollution from agriculture contributed to water quality problems in the Leet Water'.[1] In places, cattle have trampled down the bank to drink, thereby introducing the possibility of faecal contamination, a problem that will occur along the length of the watercourse whenever it is not fenced off against cattle. The Leet Water has also been affected by varying degrees of nutrient enrichment due to agricultural practices but, during the past decade, there have been substantial innovations in terms of statutory powers and non-statutory management arrangements for regulating, controlling and monitoring water quality.

The Leet Water falls within the River Tweed catchment area and is subject to the Tweed Forum's *Tweed Catchment Management Plan* (CMP), revised and updated in 2010. The Forum comprises cross-border organizations and individuals interested in the good management of the catchment area. Its CMP sets out non-statutory management proposals for the Tweed catchment under seven strategic aims covering water quality, water quantity, habitats and species, river-works, flood management, tourism and recreation and delivery and implementation of the CMP. The CMP is only part of (and provides the management framework for) an overall *Tweed Catchment Management Planning Initiative* (TCMPI), the aims of which are to 'conserve, enhance and, where appropriate, restore the total river environment through effective land and resources planning across the Tweed catchment'.

Since the launch of the CMP in 2003, the European Water Framework Directive (WFD) has been implemented which requires European Union (EU) member states to implement sustainable water resource management at the 'river basin' (or catchment) level. This in turn resulted in additional powers for the Scottish Environment Protection Agency (SEPA) through the Controlled Activities Regulations (CAR) 2005. Other EU legislation relevant to the TCMPI includes the Nitrates Directive, the Birds and Habitats Directive and the Floods Directive.

The Tweed Forum Steering Group has representation from both sides of the Border but the majority of the Tweed catchment is within Scotland where it is principally administered by Scottish Borders Council, the Scottish Environment Protection Agency (SEPA) and Scottish Natural Heritage. In terms of water quality (one of the seven CMP proposals), SEPA has objectives relating to 1. monitoring, evaluating and addressing the impact of agriculture and forestry on the water quality of the catchment, 2. minimizing the impact of residential and industrial development on the water quality of the catchment and, 3. locating, investigating and addressing specific water quality problems within the catchment. These are summary headings only and there are more specific targets within the overall objectives.

SWINTONMILL TO CHARTERPATH BRIDGE

The actions being taken by SEPA and others to reduce chemical pollution within the Tweed catchment and particularly along the Leet Water are particularly important because of the effect on fish and fishing which will be mentioned later. In their pollution reduction programme for the monitoring years 2005-2007, SEPA's description of the catchment area states:

> The Tweed has a strong nutrient gradient throughout its system, with oligotrophic [relatively low in plant nutrients with abundant oxygen] conditions in the headwaters and nutrient-rich lowlands. Land use in the upper catchment is predominantly heather and grass moorland along with significant areas of managed coniferous forestry. The rest of the catchment is dominated by arable agricultural land. The south-eastern lower parts of the catchment are designated under the Nitrates Directive as Nitrate Vulnerable Zone (NVZ) for surface and groundwater, reflecting the intensive use of land for agriculture. The Leet Water catchment, a tributary of the Tweed just upstream from sampling point 502 [at Norham], is also designated as a Surface Water NVZ.[2]

Under the same programme, SEPA has recognized the 'diffuse agricultural pollution' on the Leet Water, aggravated by land drainage schemes in the 1970s. It has undertaken a number of studies in recent years and formed a two-year action plan for the Lambden Burn, a tributary of the Leet Water, to identify significant nutrient inputs from intensive agricultural livestock and poultry units. Farmers have received grants from the Farming and Wildlife Advisory Group as a result of which four wetland or reedbed treatment systems were constructed to deal with contaminated run-off from steadings.[3]

The detailed monitoring of water quality and the scientific analysis of chemical pollutants is translating into action to improve the picture for the Leet Water. This is helped by other initiatives such as Scottish Water's £11M River Tweed Project, announced in March 2011, for the construction of six waste-water treatment works throughout the Borders. One of these is at Swinton where improvements to the Leet Water include upgrading existing equipment and providing a new pumping station and new dosing equipment. A recent visit has confirmed that this is now in place.

From Leitholm Bridge, the Leet Water flows south and then south-west to the ford west of Marlfield and the junction with the Lambden Burn which enters from the south-west. The present track linking Leitholm and Marlfield is an old one and was of greater importance in the past than it is today. It is shown quite prominently on Blackadder's map in 1797 and Crawford, in 1843, shows it as a well-defined route connecting Leitholm, Leitholm Mill and Marlfield. Leitholm Mill was a corn mill, built in the early 19th century.

Today, the track remains unsurfaced, rather overgrown in summer and used by farm vehicles, but still well-defined and a survival from times when it was routinely used as a through route. On the simple, present day map on p. 61, I have indicated part of the track by dotted lines to distinguish it as my addition to the OS base level data. I found that walking along this track and other ancient tracks along the course of the Leet Water gave me a tremendous sense of history and a feeling of time standing still.

Extract from John Blackadder's map of 1797 showing the track leading from Litholm (sic) through the ford to Marlefield (sic). Reproduced by permission of the Trustees of the National Library of Scotland.

In addition to the connections mentioned above, the track might have provided a convenient short cut across to the Coldstream road from three country houses visible on the two maps shown here—Kames, Belchester and Bughtrig. Perhaps it was also a way of avoiding the toll house at the Swintonmill crossroads! Kames was the birthplace of Henry Home (1696-1782), a distinguished judge, philosopher, sociologist and one of the leaders of the Scottish Enlightenment who became Lord Kames in 1752 and was visited by Benjamin Franklin in 1759. Lord Kames was an associate of such well-known Enlightenment figures as Adam Smith, Thomas Reid and David Hume. To Lord Kames is attributed the quotation, 'No man ever did a designed injury to another, but at the same time he did a greater to himself'.

Extract from William Crawford's and William Brooke's map of 1843 showing little change since Blackadder's map except the addition of Leitholm Mill. Reproduced by permission of the Trustees of the National Library of Scotland.

Kames House was named 'Bessborough' between 1783 and 1825, after an East India Company ship commanded by its then owner, Captain Riddell. The house has a 17th century core with later alterations and additions and is two-storey, originally a near U-plan mansion with attic comprising a symmetrical 9-bay, crowstepped and turreted block to the left and a two-storey wing to right (subsequently raised and altered) with various additions at rear. It is listed as Category A by Historic Scotland.[4] 'Kames' or 'Kaim' is Scots for a ridge, either an earthwork, or natural, such as a drumlin.

Belchester House was the seat of the Dickson family from the 14th century and the remains of the fortified house are probably incorporated in the present 18th century house. It is an asymmetrical, plain classical house comprising a two-storey, 4-bay entrance wing

68

with a classical porch, a taller, gabled wing set at right angles, forming an L-plan. There are other buildings at the rear. As with Kames, there have been many modifications and the house was probably U-shaped at the beginning of the 19th century; a fourth wing being added and the courtyard roofed over to form a larger house. A service wing and conical tower were demolished in the later part of the 20th century. The house is listed as Category B by Historic Scotland.[5] South-west of the house, is an earthwork fortification, thought to be of medieval date, comprising two banks and a ditch enclosing an oval area. Much of the defences have been damaged by later rig and furrow cultivation and the origin of the earthwork is unknown, but may have been associated with the fortified house.[6]

Bughtrig House was built in the 1780s, probably on the site of earlier buildings. It has been home to only three families since it was built, the Dicksons, the Mays and the Ramsays—Admiral Sir Bertram Ramsay, KCB, KBE, MVO, was in charge of 'Operation Dynamo', code name for the evacuation of troops from Dunkirk in 1940 and he was the Allied Naval Commander-in-Chief for the D-day landings in Normandy in 1944. The house was originally symmetrical and comprises a two-storey with basement, 3-bay classically-detailed building with later single storey and basement and 2-bay flanking wings. It is listed Category A by Historic Scotland.[7]

The photograph of Marlfield ford was taken at the end of June and shows a lush plant growth including long grasses and rushes, on either side of the Leet Water, the track and the ford, Grid Ref. NT80604453. A plant not easily seen in the bottom right hand corner of the photograph is one of the dock family (*Rumex*) and, because of

Marlfield ford, looking from east to west. There is a raised footbridge off to the right.

its long leaves with undulate margins and its position almost in the water, I think that it is probably the long-leaved dock, *Rumex longifolius,* which likes wet places and grows in the north of England and in Scotland. The traditional use of dock leaves was for treating nettle stings, although this may relate more usually to the broad-leaved dock, *Rumex obtusifolius,* which was also used for wrapping up butter. The long-leaved variety, like others, may have had limited culinary and medicinal uses and it is said that, in the Borders, long–leaved dock leaves were boiled for pig food. Another traditional livestock feed in the eastern Borders seems to have been chopped dead-nettle leaves that were formerly fed to young turkeys.[8] The bed of the Leet Water shows clear evidence of old stone surfacing (metalling). The track on the east side of the ford leads up to Marlfield farm and farmstead and beyond, to join with the Swintonmill to Coldstream road. The name of the farm is probably self-explanatory—marl was an early form of soil conditioner and fertilizer with particles of decomposed shells in the clay providing some calcareous content. This was before the more widespread use of lime as a soil dressing. In 1834, the Rev. Thomas Goldie wrote:

> Perhaps, of the whole strata visible at the surface of Coldstream parish, three quarters are composed of clay and marl. The thickness of the beds is generally inconsiderable, though in some places it may be twenty or thirty feet. It is used in some parts, where it is more calcareous than in others, for spreading over the soil; but the quantity of carbonate of lime in it is so trifling that very little benefit can be derived from the practice.[9]

It is interesting to note that Lord Henry Home Kames was a renowned land improver and the chapter headed 'Manures' in his *The Gentleman Farmer* includes much on the use of marls and lime and the techniques surrounding their use. He also states that, 'The low part of Berwickshire, termed *The Merse*, abounds everywhere with this marl; and is the only country in Scotland where it is in plenty'.[10]

Just south of Marlfield ford, the flow of the Leet Water is boosted by the Lambden Burn, which joins it from the west at Grid Ref. NT80574444. The burn is named after the hamlet and estate of Lambden near Greenlaw, meaning lamb valley (valley from the Old English *den* or *dene*).[11]

Confluence of the Lambden Burn (from left) and the Leet Water.

Immediately east of Leitholm Mill, on the Lambden Burn, crop marks have revealed a narrow ditch, forming three sides of an enclosure of unknown date.[12] The name 'Leitholm' derives from the Leet Water and the Anglo-Saxon, *ham*, meaning home or settlement.[13] Robert Gibson records that John de Lambden was the first to assume the surname from the lands of Lambden. He witnessed a charter of Robert Muscampus to William de Greenlaw about 1200. One of his descendants, Henry de Lambden, was chamberlain of Kelso Abbey for some time until 1260.[14]

South of the confluence with the Lambden Burn, the surroundings of the Leet Water change in character. Before this, the

SWINTONMILL TO CHARTERPATH BRIDGE

Leet Water runs next to or between fields and woods in a fairly narrow channel, sometimes between embankments, sometimes not. From now on, there is a valley—often with steep fields and woods and cliffs of exposed rock or soil on either side of the flood plain. The atmosphere is quite different. The stretch through Wylie Cleugh and Rough Haugh seems quite remote, although it is really quite close to nearby roads. The remoteness is emphasised by the ruined Wyliecleugh farmhouse perched above the valley and because access down into parts of the valley can be quite difficult. I thought that there were no other people about and a chance meeting with a dog walker from one of the Darnchester cottages was quite a surprise, even though this was on the way back from the valley. It was, however, a pleasant one, as we discussed local history and old maps.

Down in the valley, my unexpected presence had flushed out four roe deer, a large brown hare that rocketed up a slope and a number of pheasants. The deer had their grey winter colouring; in summer, they are orange/brown on their backs and the fauns also have attractive white spots but this turns to grey in the winter. A heron was much put out by my being there when I came round a corner just a few yards away and flapped away, noisily. A buzzard was soaring and gliding above me, giving its characteristic mewing call and a number of black-faced sheep watched my progress with suspicion.

The Leet Water meanders through Wylie Cleugh and Rough Haugh making a gurgling sound when water levels are high as it passes through gaps restricted by (when I was there) decayed vegetation remaining from the summer and autumn. However, during the shooting season, there are more people around in Wylie Cleuch and Rough Haugh, judging by the spent cartridge cases and the many small footbridges for the use of shooters and beaters.

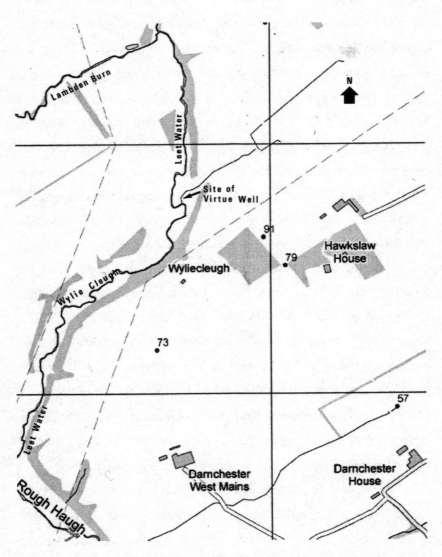

Map showing the Leet Water from the Lambden Burn through Wylie Cleugh and Rough Haugh to Darnchester. 1 km. grids. Contains Ordnance Survey data © Crown copyright and database right 2012.

Looking from Wylie Cleugh towards Rough Haugh in the distance.

The wider Leet Water in Rough Haugh. View looking downstream.

There are also livestock and tractor crossing points such as the one at the northern end of Wylie Cleugh and a more substantial bridge about halfway along Rough Haugh, opposite the woodland below Darnchester West Mains. I have taken Wylie Cleuch to be the whole valley south of the confluence of the Leet Water and the Lambden Burn down as far as Darnchester West Mains until the Leet Water swings south-east; thereafter the valley floor becomes Rough Haugh. This may not be strictly correct as the Wylie Cleugh may only apply to the area closest to the old Wyliecleugh farm. However, 'cleugh' may be defined as 'a gorge or ravine with steep rocky sides, usually the course of a stream' and, certainly, immediately after the Lambden Burn the valley becomes narrow with steep cliffs appearing on the left, continuing with other steep slopes and gullies down into Rough Haugh and beyond.[15] 'Wylie' may be a surname or it may be a corruption of some physical or natural feature—it is certainly an old component of the name and both elements appear on Blaeu's map of 1654 and Blackadder's map of 1797 with exactly the same spelling, Wyliecleuch.

The farmhouse survives as a lonely ruin—the adjoining farm buildings have been demolished and the property has not been occupied for many years. It was quite cold and windy as I tried to imagine it as it was, with a family living in it and with agricultural workers there, but the feeling of emptiness and desolation prevailed and the only sign of life was a flock of sheep huddled together in a hollow below the house.

The Leet Water also flows below Hawkslaw House and Hawkslaw farmhouse and farmstead on the east side. Hawkslaw farm

The ruined Wyliecleuch farmhouse, high above the Leet Water.

appears on Blackadder's map and both properties are named after the rounded hill (the Scots for which is *law*) on which they sit, one of the many Merse drumlins. The highest point is visible as a small, wooded enclosure which may or may not have archaeological significance, but which would provide good shelter for the hawks that still inhabit the area and are to be seen hovering and swooping on their prey. In 1895, George Muirhead thought it probable that 'Hawkslaw' was derived from an eyrie of the peregrine falcon, which also gave its name to other places in Berwickshire such as Hawksheugh near Fast Castle and Hawksheugh on the coast near Cockburnspath. He also noted that Hawkslaw was called Hawkisland in a charter by Oliver Cromwell of the Lordship and Barony of Swinton etc., dated 26th November 1656.[16]

The farm on the west side of Wylie Cleugh is Belville, close to Belchester. The RCAHMS records some carved stones that, in 1956, were reported in the *Transactions of The Berwickshire Naturalists Club* as possibly being two Roman Ionic capitals built into the walls of a farm building. It was not clear if they were still to be seen.[17]

The first edition of the 25 inch to the mile OS map, published in 1862, shows a chalybeate well called Virtue Well on the valley floor, north-west of Hawkslaw and close to where a small tributary flows down from a gulley on the east side of the Leet Water. The well is not shown on modern maps (but see the position indicated by arrow superimposed on the modern map on p. 74). In 1834, the Rev. James Thomson, Minister of Eccles wrote:

> On the borders of the parish, at the Leet, there is a chalybeate well which was furnished with a stone cover in 1780. The supply of water is pretty copious. Its sp. gr. is 1.00237 [ratio of density of the chalybeate to water], and in summer the temperature is 48d[egrees][farenheit]. The solid contents are sulphate of lime, common salt, and a minute portion of iron held in solution by carbonic acid.[18]

'Chalybeate' comes from the Latin, *chalybs* and from the Greek, *khalups*, meaning steel, referring to water containing iron salts. The name 'Virtue' derives from the virtues (benefits) that flow from drinking the water—in 1835, Dr. W. D. Robertson states 'Chalybeate mineral waters owe their virtues to the presence of either the oxide, or the carbonate, or the sulphate of iron; in their action they are tonic'.[19] However, to confuse things, there was a local surname, Virtue.[20]

Dr. Robertson refers to wells in England, such as Tunbridge Wells and one of the wells in Harrogate, but also to two wells in Scotland, the strong Moffat Water and the even stronger Vicar's Brig Chalybeate in Perthshire; he describes the latter as 'perhaps the strongest chalybeate water in the world'. This claim was confirmed by Drs. Forbes, Tweedie and Connolly in the same year, describing Vicar's Brig water as 'perhaps, the strongest in existence; at least it is the strongest which we have ever met with' and as having a specific gravity of 1.04893 from the highest reading. They mentioned the Moffat water as having a specific gravity of 1.00965 with a red colour and a sharp, astringent taste and that from the Vicar's Brig as being even harsher, four times as strong—'it could scarcely be taken into the stomach unless it were much diluted.[21] The Virtue Well was not as strong, but still stronger than Tunbridge Wells which had a recorded specific gravity of 1.0014 in 1792.

I searched for the stone-covered well, but without success. It has either disappeared or it was hidden beneath a thick and very uneven carpet of boggy, decaying grasses, sedges and rushes or, more likely, it would have been filled in during the 19th century after it ceased to be used by local people. It would be interesting to find out about what is, at present, a little piece of lost history. Did it have any spiritual rôle (there is no dedication to a Saint) like St. Antony's Well, about 1½ miles to the west at Anton's Hill? The RCAHMS record says that this is thought to have been a place of pilgrimage and healing. Its origin is unknown but there is a late 18th century stone structure, including steps down to the well and a carved stone reading FONS SACR SAN. ANTON. AC. SANITAT. Traditionally, St.

Antony's Well was said to have derived its name from the Roman Emperor.[22] However, I am straying from my route.

In connection with the morass of vegetation mentioned above, Michael Braithwaite, in his *A Botanical Tour of Berwickshire*, 2011, says 'In Rough Haugh and Wylie Cleugh there are very extensive stands of *Carex riparia* with a little *C. acuta* and *C. otrubae*. There are a few modest colonies of *Schoenoplectus lacustris* in the Leet itself or at its banks'.[23]

Carex riparia is the greater pond sedge, a clump-forming ornamental grass with brown flower spikes in early summer that requires moist or wet soil. *Carex acuta* is the acute sedge, slender tufted sedge, or slim sedge, which grows on the margins of rivers and lakes. *Schoenoplectus lacustris* or common clubrush occurs in slow-moving waters and is a very tall rush or reed-like plant with brown, egg-shaped spikelets, growing in stands in the water. Local people must have found many uses for sedges and rushes; one of the most unusual for *Carex riparia* was mentioned by George Johnston in his *The Botany of the Eastern Borders* in 1853 where he describes them as 'admirably adapted for making feet brushes for passages'.[24] These were bristles of *Carex* set and bound into beech backing boards; they were better than mats and were also surprisingly long-lasting.

The valley of the Leet Water broadens through Wylie Cleugh and into Rough Haugh, forming a much wider flood plain between the steeply rising land on either side with, generally, the more vertical slopes being on the east side. A number of small tributaries flow in from both sides until, by the time the half-way point is reached along Rough Haugh, opposite Todrig farm on the west and Darnchester

West Mains on the east, the size of the Leet Water has increased substantially, the greatest 'boost' having been supplied by the Lambden Burn.

'Todrig' is derived from the Scots *tod* meaning fox and *rig* or *rigg* meaning a ridge, such as in a ploughed, ridge and furrow field. However, the ridge could be a natural feature and Todrig is situated below a well-defined drumlin that forms a definite ridge.[25] Darnchester and Darnchester West Mains may derive partly from *deor* in Old English, meaning animal, perhaps deer. Of greater certainty is that 'chester' derives from Old Northumbrian *cæster* from Latin, *castrum*, meaning fort or camp. Whereas in England it is usually applied to Roman sites, May Williamson has suggested that this is not the case in the Scottish Border counties where it appears seventeen times, but does not once denote a Roman site.[26] The 'chester' in Darnchester may relate to the motte and bailey castle near the ruined house at Castle Law.

In the Middle Ages, the family of Darnchester or Drienchester held the land hereabouts (their seat would have been the castle) and the *Coldstream Cartulary* records gifts that were made during the 13th century to Coldstream Priory. For example:

> Walter, son of Sir Thomas of Darnchester, with the consent of his heirs granted them twelve acres of land in 'Huysheuigh', and twelve acres in Old Hirsel that is 7 acres in one cultura (an area of cultivation) and 5 acres in another, in pure and perpetual alms. Walter, chaplain, gave one toft [Scots: a homestead and its land] and croft within the villa of Darnchester from the east of the road called 'Cakewellgat', to

make a pittance to the nuns on the morrow of St. Lawrence the martyr, in free, pure and perpetual alms with common pasture in the villa of Darnchester and all common easements within and outwith the villa. He also gave with the consent of Walter, son of Siward, his father $1^1/_2$ acres of land above 'Coteflatte' from the east of the land, '...?', in pure and perpetual alms. Richard, son of Hugh, cook of Darnchester gave one toft in the villa of Darnchester with one rod next to the toft rendering for all service one pound of cumin or three half-pennies at the Fair at Roxburgh. Alan, son of Thomas, son of Elena, gave $1^1/_2$ acres of land west of his croft, with a toft and three acres called 'Spitelflat' in the territory of Darnchester, in pure, free and perpetual alms. He also gave one acre of land in the villa of Darnchester lying next to the road called 'Cakewellgat' towards the east, rendering 1d. or a pair of gloves at the feast of St. James the apostle in the name of feu ferme for all services.[27]

These were only some of the many gifts and grants of land in the 13th century recorded in the *Coldstream Cartulary*, allowing the priory to gain and maintain considerable wealth and influence before its destruction by the Earl of Hertford in 1545 and its dissolution in 1587.

The medieval *Coldstream Cartulary* was published by the Grampian Club (ed. C. Rogers) in 1879. The Club, along with a number of other Gentlemen's Clubs, had restricted membership and edited and printed many works relating to Scottish history and antiquities. The Club's Patron was H.R.H. The Prince of Wales.

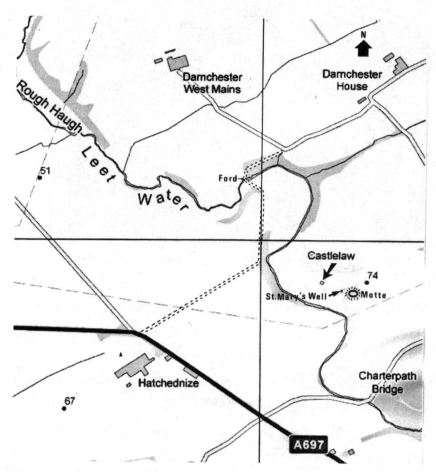

Map showing the Leet Water from Rough Haugh to Charterpath Bridge. 1 km. grid lines. Contains Ordnance Survey data © Crown copyright and database right 2012.

Ownership and occupation of the Darnchester farms and 'township' together with the motte and bailey castle and the house at Castle Law, have passed through many hands since that time. At Darnchester, there is a ford across the Leet Water (Grid Ref.

Darnchester ford from the north-west, showing the ruined footbridge.

NT80934224) that must have given a useful connection to the main road (now A697/A68) to Edinburgh. The ford and unsurfaced track are superimposed on the above map by dotted lines but the track is shown prominently on Blackadder's map in the 18th century and also on Crawford's map in the early 19th century; however, the ford must have been impassable quite often at this point on the Leet Water, when this was in spate. When I was there, in summer, the water level was low and the ford was passable with ease, particularly as there is now a firm, concrete base to the ford. The footbridge had ceased to be of any use but I didn't need it anyway. It was a pleasant spot, more open on the upstream side with trees set back and fields beyond but enclosed on the downstream side with trees overhanging the ever-widening Leet Water. One of my favourite trees, a common beech, *Fagus sylvatica*, was right on the ford. Known as 'The Lady of the

Woods' because of its graceful appearance, smooth, silver-grey trunk and delicate leaves, the beech was always a useful countryside resource; it burnt well as fuel and it was useful for making furniture.

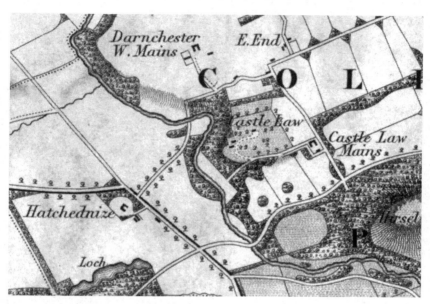

Extract from William Crawford's and William Brooke's map of 1843 showing the Darnchester track and ford and the surrounding area. Reproduced by permission of the Trustees of the National Library of Scotland.

Downstream from Darnchester ford, the Leet Water sweeps around in a double loop below the land of Castlelaw Farm, the ruined house at Castle Law (described as The Castle on the modern OS Explorer map) and the earthworks of the motte and bailey castle (see the map on p. 83). Neither Blackadder nor Crawford depict the motte and bailey on their maps but an earlier map by A. and M. Armstrong in 1771 clearly shows it, described as 'Mount'.[28] The flood plain of the Leet Water remains wide but with even steeper sides until it nears

Charterpath Bridge; the scene is quite dramatic but the rough, marshy ground of Wyliecleugh and Rough Haugh is replaced by smooth turf up the east slopes and over the sites of Castle Law house and the motte and bailey. The short turf results from close cropping by sheep.

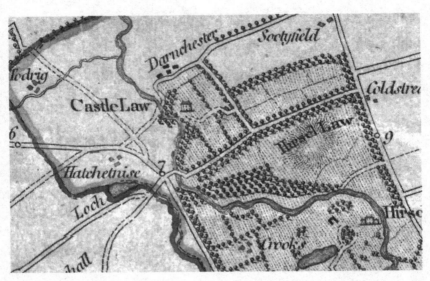

Extract from John Blackadder's map of 1797 showing the house at Castle Law and the tree-lined policies. Charterpath Bridge is to the east of No. 7 on the map. Reproduced by permission of the Trustees of the National Library of Scotland.

The ruined house at Castle Law (Grid Ref. NT81204191) may be a 17th century house with 18th century additions, possibly incorporating structures from the 16th century or even earlier. At some time, the owners of the Darnchester estate must have decided that the 12th century castle on the nearby motte was no longer suitable for occupation and decided to build a new structure at Castle Law.

In the 17th century, the Trotter family must have held the estate because, in April 1648, the Records of the Parliament of

86

Scotland show an Edward Trotter of Darnchester listed as one of the colonels of horse and foot 'for the shirefdome of Berwik' under an 'Act of posture anent the putting of the kingdom in ane posture of warr for defence'.[29] This was just after the start of the Second Civil War in March 1648, when there were Royalist uprisings in England and Wales (which were crushed by Cromwell and Fairfax) and just before the Scots army was mobilized in May, so the Parliamentary records reflect a very insecure time.

The ruined house at Castle Law viewed from the south-west.

The Ainslie family were at Darnchester, whether as owners or occupiers of all or part of the estate, for some period until the middle of the 18th century when Robert Ainslie, W.S. moved to Berrywell near Duns to become factor to Lord Douglas.[30] In 1838, in a Supreme

Court case, the estate of Darnchester was described as consisting 'of four portions, two of which belonged to the late James Rocheid of Inverleith'. These were sold in 1784 and 1797 'to one, Waite' and were later sold on to others and eventually, in 1838, to Dickson of Chatto. The two portions seem to have been extensive, comprising:

> the croft of land called Baillie Croft, the lands called the common of Darnchester, and others, with houses, biggings [buildings, dwellings], yards, parts, pendicles [adjuncts] and pertinents of the same...[31]

The 'Waite' mentioned above would be William Waite, who is listed as having his seat at Castle Law, in an undated, but post-1792 pocket travel directory describing the landowners along the road from Coldstream to Edinburgh.[32] In 1797-8, he had eight horses, all of them taxable under the Horse Tax, at a payment of 16s. 0d. Under the Clock and Watch Tax, he paid 13s. $1^{1}/_{2}$d, in respect of one clock, one gold watch and one metal watch. [33]

The 'New' Statistical Account of Scotland 1834, refers to the seat of a Professor Russell at Castlelaw and the 1836 list of Land Tax Commissioners for the Shire of Berwick gives the names of Dr. James Russel (sic) of Castlelaw and Dr. James Russel (sic) younger, of Castlelaw.[34]

The RCAHMS record for Castle Law describes the ruinous state of the two-storey building in detail and refers to its depiction on the 1st edition of the OS 6-inch map that shows an unroofed extension to the south-east and further ranges around a courtyard to the north-east. The OS Object Name Book in 1861 describes the building as 'A good stone building two storeys high with out offices, a garden,

orchard and arable farm attached. Proprietor Arch. Dickson, Esq.'
There was also a cottage known as Castlelaw Gardens which still
survives as does the 'arable farm', Castlelaw farm, but the extensions,
outbuildings, gardens and orchards have all gone, leaving the sheep to
graze all around the windswept ruins.[35]

South-east of Castle Law is the Armstrongs' 'Mount',
mentioned earlier on p. 85. This is the surviving motte of a probable
12th century motte and bailey castle that must have been occupied by
the Darnchester family and others until it was replaced by a castle or
fortified house at Castle Law; this, in turn, was replaced on the same
site by the present ruined house. The RCAHMS record states that the
bailey is only visible in crop marks on air photographs that show that
it measured about 105m. from east to west by 75m. transversely
within double ditches on the south and east sides with steep, natural
slopes on the north and west sides (above the Leet Water). There was
an entrance near the south-east corner. The motte and bailey were
inspected by RCAHMS in 1908, 1955, 1966, 1978 and 2008. In 1862,
the OS Object Name Book described the motte as 'A small hillock or
mound having a tabulated summit and surrounded by a slight fosse;
the whole being studded with wood'. The trees were still there in
1955 but had gone by 1966.[36]

The motte itself, which is in the north-east corner of the
former bailey at Grid Ref. NT81424182, was described in 1978 as
standing to a maximum height of 16m. above the bottom of a broad,
encircling ditch with a flat top of 20m. in diameter. By 2008, sheep
had eroded an area near the summit on the south-west side and there
are now several bare areas showing the sand and gravel construction.

89

The motte and ditch looking south-east from near Castle Law house.

The ditch has been filled in two places on the west-south-west and south-east sides, forming causeways. In 1955, the RCAHMS could find no trace of any masonry either on top of the motte or in a small trench that had been cut into the top edge on the south side. Originally, the motte would have been surmounted by a wooden tower with a surrounding wooden palisade but it was probably not replaced by any stone building; instead it seems the decision was taken to relocate to Castle Law. However, such speculation would need archaeological confirmation.

So far, there has not been any evidence of Roman activity anywhere on the strategic heights of Castle Law despite Roman presence in the area. Dere Street, the permanent fort at Trimontium and other temporary camps were nearby. There must also have been two-way trading with the 'friendly' British tribe of the Votadini.

On the south-south-east side of The Mount is a stone slab described by the RCAHMS as:

> A stone slab standing to a height of about 80cm. situated on the outer part of the causeway at the SSE edge. On the S-facing side is an inscription with a double lined circle. The faded description is difficult to read, but is likely to read 'St. Margaret's' the second line reads 'walk'.[37]

The Coldstream Gateway Charitable Trust website suggests that the walk is 'no doubt named after Wait's [sic] wife Margaret...'[38] This would be Margaret, the wife of the owner of Castle Law, William Waite. Margaret's memorial stone is on the north wall of Lennel kirkyard and reads, 'Margaret Dysart died 12 December 1813 wife of William Waite Esq. of Castle Law'.[39]

At the side of the track that passes between Castle Law and The Mount and leads down to the cottage and the flood plain of the Leet Water, is another well, St. Mary's well, at Grid Ref. NT81354186. The RCAHMS, which defines a well (as opposed to a tapped, natural spring) as 'a shaft sunk into the ground to provide a supply of water', records its details as:

> 'A spring well, faced with masonry and having a stone erected on it bearing its name. It was named St. Mary's Well by Mr. Wait [sic], a former proprietor, in commemoration of one of his relatives, a benevolent and pious young lady'.[40]

The well was listed as a 'Holy Well' by J. Russel Walker, architect, in 1883. He put forward 'a possible origin for Holy Wells in Scotland'

St. Mary's Well, Castle Law; The St. Margaret's Walk stone is behind.

based upon an account in Adamnan's (ninth abbot of Iona) *Life of St. Columba* written in the 7th century:

> Whilst the blessed man [St. Columba] was stopping for some days in the province of the Picts, he heard that there was a fountain famous among this heathen people, which foolish men, having their senses blinded of the devil, worshipped as a god. For those who drank this fountain, or purposely washed their hands or feet in it, were allowed by God to be struck by demoniacal art, and went home either leprous or purblind, or at least suffering from weakness or other kinds of infirmity. By all these things the pagans were seduced and paid divine honours to the fountain. Having ascertained this, the saint one

day went up to the fountain fearlessly, and on seeing this, the Druids, whom he had often sent away vanquished and confounded, were greatly rejoiced, thinking that, like others, he would suffer from the touch of the baneful waters. The saint then blessed the fountain, and from that day the demons separated from the water; and not only was it not allowed to injure any one, but even many diseases amongst the people were cured by this same fountain after it had been blessed and washed in by the saint.[41]

There seem to have been more wells dedicated to the Virgin Mary than to any other saint and J. R. Walker believed that many of the well offerings, prayers and supplications were associated with overcoming female sterility. Offerings may have been pebbles, sometimes a coin, scraps of clothing, or even rags. The church authorities eventually tried to prevent worship and, in 1579, a statute was passed prohibiting pilgrimage to wells, backed up in 1629 by a Privy Council denunciation. However, superstition prevailed, although visits had to be made by stealth, perhaps at night.

Below Castle Law and The Mount, the Leet Water sweeps round in a wide loop between the short-cropped grass on the east and north-east banks and a narrow belt of trees on the west and south-west banks. Behind the tree belt are arable fields. At the steep embankment below the site of the bailey, the Leet Water changes direction to the south-west before swinging round to the south and south-east to pass under the modern Charterpath Bridge at Grid Ref. NT81434132. The bridge replaces an earlier bridge and carries the unclassified road that runs south-westwards along the side of Dunglass Wood, linking Duns

Road near Hirsel Law with the A697 road, south-east of Hatchednize. The earlier bridge must have been built between 1771 and 1797, as it is shown on Blackadder's map (see p. 86) but not on Armstrong's 1771 map that shows a ford at this point. The origin of the name, 'Charterpath' is unknown, but it may have a connection with one of the medieval charters transferring land to Coldstream Priory that are held in the *Coldstream Cartulary*. Some of these were mentioned earlier (see pp. 81-2) but land in the vicinity of the present bridge, at and around The Hirsel, was also granted to the priory by Patrick, Earl of Dunbar and other members of his family in the 13th century.[42]

The early summer scene, looking north from the bridge, is pleasantly pastoral, despite some rock armouring to the banks on the bridge approaches and the 'Armco' barrier alongside the road. However, the views in summer on both sides of Charterpath Bridge show that the tranquil and slow-moving Leet Water is allowing a build-up of algae. A small amount of algae can be beneficial to rivers by photosynthesizing sunlight and releasing oxygen into the water. The danger is that a high concentration of nitrates and phosphates can cause what is known as eutrophication resulting in excessive amounts of algae that consume large quantities of oxygen from the water overnight, leading to suffocation of fish and other creatures. There are several species of algae found in Scottish fresh waters including the blue-green algae, *Cyanophyta* or *Cyanobacteria*, the green algae, *Chlorophyta* and the yellow-brown algae, *Chrysophyta*.

The blue-green algae species can be quite toxic and its presence would not be conducive to the return of the freshwater mussel, *Margaritifera margaritifera* that used to live amongst the

Looking north, upstream, from Charterpath Bridge.

gravels and pebbles of the Leet Water after spending its larval stage attached to the gills of salmonid fish. In historic times, freshwater mussels were destroyed for their pearls somewhere above Charterpath Bridge but mussels may now be extinct in the Leet Water. This was primarily due to overfishing from the 18th century onwards as it was necessary to destroy large numbers of mussels in order to find one with a pearl inside. Although local people have recollections of mussels being in the Leet, subsequent agricultural pollution would have completed their demise. Since 1981, it has been illegal throughout Scotland to intentionally kill, injure, take or disturb freshwater pearl mussels or damage their habitat. Amending legislation in 1998 also made it illegal to possess mussels and pearls collected after that date or to sell them or advertise their sale unless done under licence from Scottish Natural Heritage.[43]

The course of the Leet Water from Swintonmill to Charterpath Bridge has been a fascinating stretch. The scenery of the valley and the land on either side is varied and sometimes quite dramatic. There are woods and fields, marshes, bogs and cliffs, overhanging trees on steep-sided slopes and windswept vistas above and below. The valley winds its way along, sometimes in broad sweeps and sometimes in narrower loops, but the Leet Water, which is gaining in strength all the time, is not content to follow an easy route within its confines but, instead, twists and turns, in what can only be described as a 'crinkly' manner.

There is an atmosphere of timelessness and everywhere there is a sense of history; sometimes this is highly visible in the case of The Mount, the derelict and ruined Castle Law House, the Wylie Cleugh farmhouse and the nearby country houses, but there is also a feeling that this is an old landscape that has been fought over and farmed for thousands of years. People have lived on the land, they have tended it, they have used it and they have travelled over it; they have drawn water from the Leet Water and the Virtue Well and they have made offerings at or looked for comfort from, St. Mary's Well. Their successors are still here, providing continuity.

5

The Hirsel

Below Charterpath Bridge, the character of the landscape changes again. From here, until the Leet Water passes under the bridge carrying the A698 road at Coldstream, the country is more wooded than before and, because this stretch is entirely within the parkland and agricultural setting of The Hirsel estate, there are no settlements other than where the Leet Water runs alongside the outskirts of Coldstream for half a mile on its north-east side. Even then, the areas of housing and playing fields are high above the Leet Water and are screened by dense woodland that preserves the 'green corridor'. The only other buildings are those associated with the estate including The Hirsel house, former stables, a number of cottages and lodges, the Homestead including the craft units, museum and tearoom and The Hirsel Golf Club.

The Hirsel estate extends to approximately 3,000 acres and is the seat of the Earls of Home; it has been in the family ownership since 1611 when the barony was purchased from the Kers of Littledean, Maxton, in Roxburghshire. The house is listed Category A and there are records to show that the architect, William Adam, was responsible for alterations in 1739-41. He added a north-east wing and carried out works to the earlier tower. The architect, William Atkinson, altered the building in 1813-15 and built on a wing, but his work was incorporated into another scheme by William Burn that was completed in about 1818. David Bryce made further alterations in 1858, James Campbell Walker made others and George Henderson also did so in 1897. Ian Lindsay supervised the demolition of a Victorian wing and chapel in 1958-9. The Homestead and Doocot were built in about 1800, Montague Lodge and the Keeper's Cottage and Kennels in 1853 and 1894, respectively and the stables in 1900. The walled garden was probably built in the mid-18th century.[1]

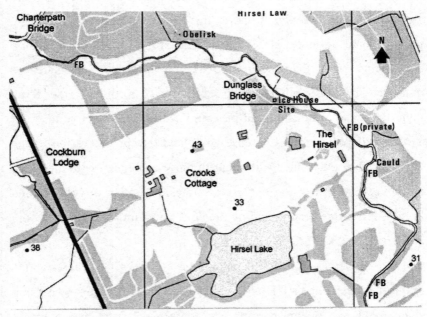

Map showing a small part of The Hirsel estate with the Leet Water flowing in a variety of directions from Charterpath Bridge, passing below Hirsel Law, then below The Hirsel house and around the woods and fields to the east of Hirsel Lake. 1 km. grid lines. Contains Ordnance Survey data © Crown copyright and database right 2012.

THE HIRSEL

Crawford's map of 1843 shows neither Cockburn Lodge nor Montague Lodge at the entrance to Montague Avenue leading from the Edinburgh Road to The Hirsel house. It does show the avenue shadowing the course of the Leet Water as far as the house. It still does, but it is probable that the avenue had greater prominence at one time than it does now. Today, the main access to the house and estate is from the A698 road at Coldstream. In earlier times, it would have been more convenient for carriages coming from Edinburgh to have approached the house via the Montague Lodge entrance. Whereas the modern approach now has a bitumen surface, the northern approach retains its 'metalled' but unsealed state.

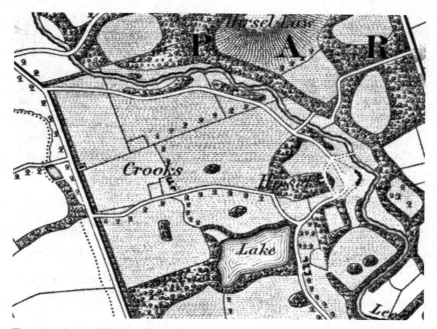

Extract from William Crawford's and William Brooke's map of 1843 showing the same, small part of The Hirsel estate. Reproduced by permission of the Trustees of the National Library of Scotland.

Some idea of the former status of the avenue may be obtained by the row of five Wellingtonia, *Sequoiadendron giganteum*, that were planted alongside the carriage drive of Montague Avenue at one point. Their full glory would not have been visible until long after they were planted; this would probably be between 1850 and 1860.

Footbridge (see below) showing old stonework on the north bank.

South-east of Charterpath Bridge, the Leet Water flows between a wood on the left side and a field to the right before turning east and entering a wood within which it is spanned by a footbridge at Grid Ref. NT81654121. On the north bank, the bridge leads by footpaths to extensive woodland, within which is a reservoir and an obelisk (map, p. 98) and then onwards to Dunglass Wood and Hirsel Law. Whereas the timber boarding and handrails of the bridge are

100

now carried on rolled steel joists, originally there would have been a stone bridge, as evidenced by the surviving bridge supports and abutments, particularly on the north side. The style of construction with the three round flood arches made me think that this must have been an 18th century construction although the bridge does not feature on Crawford's map. It can be seen on the 1862 1st edition OS map with a ford downstream; there was also a well on the south side.

Below the footbridge (marked FB on map, p.98), the Leet Water flows into more open ground but still with rising woodland on the north bank. The valley floor is thick with course grassland and marsh plants but this vista is the first opportunity to see the wide variety of native and exotic trees planted on the Hirsel estate. Historic Scotland provides a concise description of the woodland:

> The Hirsel has been recorded in the past as having the largest concentration of deciduous woodland and coniferous plantation in the Merse. Some of the woodland, especially Dunglass Wood, was planted before 1750; others such as Dundock Wood were planted in the late 18th century by the 10th Earl and these plantations can be seen on the 1841 Blackadder survey. Many of the woodland blocks suffered in the gale of 1881 and what remained of Dundock Wood had to be completely underplanted by rhododendrons and azaleas. The woodland strips of beech and oak along the banks of the Leet were planted as ornamental woodland in c. 1800. Today, some of the older oak and beech are overmature but the later planting, probably mid-19th century, includes trees such as horse chestnuts, Wellingtonias, white firs, Douglas fir, Scots

pine and Norway spruce. Kincham Wood was clear felled during World War II and part of Dunglass and Kincham Woods have been replanted with mixed-aged small blocks of conifers with single species, or only a few varieties.[2]

There are many individual ancient, veteran and notable trees that have special significance, such as the 'Flodden tree' the 'Coronation oak' of 1902 and the tulip tree in the walled garden; there are also special plantings such as the 105 trees gifted by the Foreign and Commonwealth Office to Sir Alec Douglas-Home on his 70th birthday in 1973, representing all the countries that he had visited in office.[3]

The importance of the woodland and wildlife habitats along the Leet Water south-east of Charterpath Bridge almost as far as the outskirts of Coldstream is such that the area forms one part (the other part being The Hirsel Lake, surrounding woodland strips and Dundock Wood) of The Hirsel Site of Special Scientific Interest (SSSI) which is protected under legislation, the most recent being the Nature Conservation (Scotland) Act 2004. The site was designated and is monitored by Scottish Natural Heritage whose ongoing site management statements emphasise the large area of mixed habitats and the diversity of species and high wildlife population.

The whole site is home to breeding and passage/wintering birds unequalled elsewhere in the Scottish Borders including species that are rare in Scotland. More than 91 species of breeding birds include kingfisher, yellow wagtail, hawfinch, goosander, dipper, sand martin, water rail, lesser whitethroat, pied flycatcher, willow tit and marsh tit. The wintering species include goosander, whooper swan, mallard, shoveler and mute swan. In 2009, there was concern that breeding bird species were in decline but subsequent reviews suggest that this could be reversed by various practical land management measures in order to maintain and enhance the habitats.

Plant species with only local distribution in Scotland include greater pond sedge *Carex riparia*, water betony *Scophularia auriculata*, wall lettuce *Mycelis muralis*, horned pondweed *Zannichellia palustris* and hornwort *Ceretophyllum demersum*. A nationally rare species, green figwort *Scrophularia umbrosa*, has been recorded here. Scottish Natural Heritage note that more than 140 flowering plants, grasses and ferns have been recorded on the site.[4]

Above the trees on the left in the photograph, is a large open-topped hill of about 3.7 ha. (9.14 acres) with only a fenced plantation of pheasant cover and feed crop interrupting the grassy summit. This is Hirsel Law at Grid Ref. NT82524160. The RCAHMS record says that this is the site of a hill fort and that crop marks on air photographs in 1977 revealed one or possibly two ditches 'following the contours of this gentle, whale-backed ridge'; these are not visible at ground level.[5] The size of the fort puts it in the class of 'minor oppida' in archaeological terms. Although the Latin *oppidum* means town, in this situation it does not imply a town in the urban sense but rather, a fortified settlement. The record does not give a date for the age of the hill fort and does not note any excavation of the site. The view from the top is impressive, a good vantage point for a fort. The weather on this winter day was clear but cold with a strong wind whistling across the top and we soon left. The Trig. Point is at 94m. (308ft.) but the summit is a short distance to the north-east and a metre or so higher.

Looking south from the Trig. Point on Hirsel Law towards Hirsel Lake and the Cheviot Hills.

Below Hirsel Law and overlooking the Leet Water is the obelisk mentioned on p. 100 which was erected by the 9th Earl of Home in 1784 in memory of his elder son, William, Lord Dunglass who, as a lieutenant in the Coldstream Guards, died of wounds, aged 24, after the battle of Guilford Courthouse in December 1781 in the American War of Independence. The British were victorious in the battle but suffered such heavy casualties that it was regarded as a *pyrrhic* victory. The obelisk with a semi-circle of contemporary yew trees is sited in a small clearing overlooking the Leet Water and is highly visible from Montague Avenue on the far side—a permanent reminder of the tragedy and a poignant memorial.

Opposite the obelisk is a small footbridge, not part of the public footpath network, but used for estate management purposes. A few hundred metres downstream, the Leet Water is crossed by Dunglass Bridge, suitable for agricultural vehicles and pedestrians.

Dunglass Bridge from the west.

The bridge was built in 1948 as a replacement for an earlier stone bridge built in 1829, (as evidenced by a carved stone plaque). This would have been during the lifetime of Alexander Ramey-Home, 10th Earl of Home (1769-1841). The floods in August 1948 caused one of the worst disasters ever to hit Berwickshire; a third of the annual rainfall fell in six days causing widespread damage to property. All the rivers burst their banks and Coldstream's Market Square and surrounding streets were under water. The destruction of

105

Dunglass Bridge on what is only a small tributary of the Tweed is evidence of the scale and power of the floods. The new bridge is an important crossing point, not just for the family and their estate workers but also for the many walkers who use the marked trails on The Hirsel estate.

A notice on the bridge gives an illustrated account of the life cycle of the brown trout. It also describes the 'Leet Water Habitat Project':

> The Leet was once renowned for the quality of its Brown Trout Fishing with fish up to three pounds not uncommon. It is also a valuable nursery stream providing stocks of young Trout for the Tweed. Intensification of agriculture in the catchment including drainage works in the 1970s and heavy grazing pressure has reduced the quality of habitat for the Trout and a wide range of other riverside wildlife. As part of the Tweed Rivers Heritage Project which is part funded by the Heritage Lottery Fund and a wide range of partners, the Coldstream & District Angling Association in conjunction with Douglas & Angus Estates and the Tweed Foundation have fenced this section of the Leet to allow natural streamside vegetation to develop supplemented by native tree & shrub planting. In time, this will improve conditions for juvenile and adult Trout by enhancing spawning and nursery areas and by providing increased cover for resident adult fish.

As regards fishing, the Leet Water can no longer be considered in isolation as it, along with other tributaries, forms part of the strictly regulated and administered River Tweed system. The Leet Water needs the conservation work that it is receiving in order to nurture stocks. In the past, there were not the same problems with pollution and many large trout could be caught. For example, in 1892, (but referring to earlier in the 19th century) Thomas Tod Stoddart wrote:

> Of all streams that I am acquainted with, the Leet, which discharges itself into the Tweed above Coldstream, was wont, considering its size, to contain the largest trout...Not many years ago, the whole course of it was infested with pike, but the visit of some otters, irrespective of the angler's art, has completely cleared them out, and thus allowed the trout, which were formerly scarce, to become more numerous.
>
> On the first occasion of my fishing Leet, which happened to be early in April, before the sedge and rushes had assumed the ascendancy, I captured with the fly twenty-six trout, weighing in all upwards of twenty-nine pounds. Of these, five at least were two-pounders, and there were few, if any, small-sized fish. On the 2nd day of June, the weather being bright and hot, I killed with the worm, out of the same stretch of water, betwixt Castlelaw and Boughtrig [sic], forty-two trout, weighing upwards of twenty-three pounds; also, on a similar day in June, betwixt ten and two o'clock in the forenoon, I managed to encreel three dozen and five fish, the largest of which was a three-pounder, and there were at least twelve others that weighed a pound a-piece. The gross weight on this occasion I neglected to take note of, but it certainly approached two stone.[6]

Today, the River Tweed Commission has the responsibility under the

Scotland Act 1998 (River Tweed) Order 2006 for the preservation of salmon, sea trout, brown trout and other freshwater fish in the River Tweed and its tributaries (and extending five miles out to sea), the regulation of fisheries, the removal of nuisances and obstructions and the prevention of illegal fishing. It also has a very detailed policy on fish stocking. The Commission receives the advice and assistance of the Tweed Committee whose members represent the fishing interests of the Lower, Middle and Upper Tweed, the main tributaries, the netting interests, the angling associations, non-proprietory commissioners and the Tweed Foundation.

The Tweed Commission retains responsibility for policing and administration and delegates the scientific aspects of stock management to the Tweed Foundation through The Tweed Fisheries Management Plan. The Tweed Foundation was set up in 1983 and is a charitable trust with the trustees tasked to promote the development of salmon and trout stocks throughout the Tweed system through biological research, stock monitoring and habitat enhancement.

A distinction has to be made between salmon fishing rights that are quite separate from land ownership and can be bought and sold on their own—and other fishing rights, e.g. trout fishing rights, ownerships of which are tied to the land and pass on when that land is sold to a new owner. There are salmon fishing rights on the Leet Water in private ownership and in the ownership of the Crown Estate but, effectively, there is no salmon fishing because salmon only go to the Leet to spawn and it is illegal to catch the young salmon parr (salmon eggs hatch into 'fry' that develop into 'parr' for the first two years or so of their life before becoming 'smolts' that are able to live

Looking downstream from Dunglass Bridge.

in sea water). It is legal to fish other species subject to ownership of the rights. There is no ownership of fish, merely of the right to fish.

109

LEET WATER FROM SOURCE TO TWEED

There are no longer any pike in the Leet Water and Stoddart confirms that these were no longer there in his day (say from the 1840s onwards); nor are there any grayling. There are salmon parr, brown trout, sea trout, minnows and lampreys in the Leet Water and, in 2011, the Tweed Foundation's senior biologist reported that, for the first time, salmon fry had been found at two sites on the Lambden Burn—evidence that spawning is now taking place in the upper Leet. This is an indication that there is an improvement in water quality.[7] The salmon fishing season runs from 1st February to 30th November.

Three species of lamprey are found in Scotland, the brook lamprey, *Lampetra planeri*, the river lamprey, *Lamprey fluviatilis* and the sea lamprey, *Petromyzon marinus*, the sea lamprey being the largest of the species, reaching up to one metre in length. They resemble eels in having a long, cylindrical body; they have a skeleton of cartilage, no fish scales, a single nostril on top of the head, seven sac-like gills opening on each side of the head and primitive mouthparts surrounded by a flexible lip that acts as a sucker—hence the scientific name for the sea lamprey, *Petromyzon*, meaning stone sucker. The brook lamprey is an entirely freshwater species growing to a length of 15-19cm, whereas the river lamprey migrates from its coastal feeding grounds into fresh water for spawning and can grow to 30-50cm. Most species of lamprey are parasitic and feed on other fish.

The trout, *Salmo trutta*, to be found in the Leet Water, has two alternative life cycles. The first is the freshwater form known as brown trout and the second is the sea trout, which is not a separate species but a migratory form of the brown trout with a life cycle similar to the Atlantic salmon, *Salmo salar*, in that it migrates to sea

110

in order to feed and grow and then returns to fresh water to spawn. The brown trout does have a migratory pattern but it spends all of its life in fresh water.[8] Trout fishing runs from 15th March to 6th October.

A great deal of work has been done to improve the water quality of the Leet Water as a tributary of the River Tweed by limiting the run-off of agricultural chemicals and protecting the Leet Water as an important spawning ground and habitat for salmon and trout. This has been work done by estate owners and farmers and organizations such as SEPA, the Tweed Commission, the Tweed Foundation, Scottish Borders Council and wildlife and environmental agencies such as Scottish Natural Heritage. The information board at Dunglass Bridge, quoted on p. 106, refers to the partnership between Coldstream & District Angling Association, the Tweed Foundation and Douglas & Angus Estates that came about in 2000 to improve the natural habitat of brown trout in the Leet Water. It was an opportune moment because, in 1999, the Tweed Rivers Heritage Project was set up involving a number of organisations under the umbrella of the Tweed Forum (set up in 1991). The aim of the project was:

> to conserve, enhance and raise awareness of the natural, built and cultural heritage of the rivers and valleys of the Tweed catchment and develop the recreational opportunities and quality of life.

It was suggested that the work of the Tweed Foundation, The Hirsel estate and Coldstream & District Angling Association should be part of the Tweed Rivers Heritage Project. The work involved fencing off the Leet Water wherever possible through the estate and the planting of native trees and shrubs.[9] (See note for species). It was necessary because cattle had worn down the banks over the years and destroyed vegetation that acted as shelter and a food supply for the trout. The fencing and planting would provide 'buffer' zones inaccessible to the cattle and would also protect habitats for wildlife, including otters.

The project was successful in obtaining European Leader funding of £6,000 subject to a guarantee of a twenty years life, a commitment from Douglas & Angus Estates and a lease to Coldstream & District Angling Association. Match funding involved the provision of labour needed to carry out the project. In 2002, the project was also successful in winning a £500 runners-up conservation award from the Wild Trout Trust.

Below Dunglass Bridge, the Leet Water flows in a generally south-east direction with occasional switches to the south-west as it passes The Hirsel house, home to David, the 15th Earl of Home, son of the 14th Earl who, as Prime Minister, was Sir Alec Douglas-Home. The Leet Water also passes to the east of The Hirsel lake, an artificial, ornamental lake created in 1786, that has an area of 27 acres and is one of the few 'lakes' rather than 'lochs' in Scotland. The lake was stocked with pike and, in 1834, it was stated that these were 'of a very large size, sometimes weighing upwards of 32 lbs'.[10] Now the lake is at the heart of The Hirsel Country Park and is surrounded by reed beds providing cover for wildlife; there is a hide for bird-watchers to view mute swan, whooper swan, moorhen, little grebe, heron, pochard, shoveler, tufted duck, goosander, reed bunting, sedge warbler and many other species (some listed on p.102 in connection with the SSSI), at different times of the year.

Just to the side of the 'carriage drive' of Montague Avenue

and north-west of The Hirsel house, there is the site of a former ice-house which can only be identified by a hollow in the ground and a few blocks of stone at Grid Ref. NT82694097 (see map, p. 98). The ice-house was in woodland above the Leet Water on its south-west side where there is a steep slope down to the haugh. It does not appear on Crawford's map of 1843 but can be clearly seen on the OS Six-inch 1st edition map of 1862. The building did not last long having been demolished in 1889. In 1853, Charles McIntosh describes the site as having 'a high, dry, airy situation, having a northern exposure, and partly shaded with large trees'. As for the structure:

> A pit, 14 feet square and the same depth, was excavated and lined round with course boarding; a well, 5 or 6 feet deep, dug under this for the melted ice to drain into; and from this well a leaden pipe is carried up to a convenient part, to which a pump is attached, so that any water accumulating in the well may be pumped up...This well is covered by laying some strong planks across it; and these, covered with faggots [tied bundles of sticks], form the base for the ice to rest on, and...to keep the bottom always dry. In each corner of the pit a strong post is fixed, upon which a roof is placed 4 feet above the surface of the ground. The space from the ground to the springing of the roof is boarded with slabs, having a door in the north side, in which a sliding ventilator is fixed, and another ventilator is placed in the opposite side...The roof is thatched from 18 inches to 2 feet in thickness; the eaves project above 2 feet, to prevent the sun from acting on the sides...[11]

Lady Caroline Douglas-Home has found the only reference to

the ice-house in The Hirsel archives, in The Hirsel Factory Account for the year ending 10 November 1889, for refreshments to

Fig. 728.

the men filling it in. She remembers that, in 1959, it was possible to see part of some corrugated iron sheeting that had been placed over the infill to take leaf-mould. Also, the entrance on the north side was just discernable—today some stone blocks are still visible that may have been part of the threshold foundations. Fig 728 shows McIntosh's drawing of the ice-house.

A footpath from The Hirsel house leads down to a footbridge over the Leet Water within the private policies of the house and then north-east to meet the public footpath from Dunglass Bridge. Downstream from here, there is a stone 'cauld' in the bed of the Leet Water at Grid Ref. NT83104071. This is like a weir or small dam that, at one time, would have diverted water into a lade to serve one or more corn mills on the east side of the Leet Water north of the Leet Bridge at Coldstream. The evidence for more than one mill can be seen in the extent of the surviving, if incomplete, lades that are still traceable alongside the present footpaths from the cauld and almost as far as Coldstream. Documents also suggest more than one mill on the Leet Water (not including the now demolished Lees Mill at the Leet

Bridge which was built much later).

The private Act of Parliament that transferred the priory of Coldstream and all its lands to Sir John Hamilton of Trabrown, Earl of Melrose in 1621, includes in the transfer:

> The Manis of Cauldstreame...and...land in the toun and territorie of Hirsell, Vulgo Lie, Countes Croft, Cauldstremeflett and pece land lyand besyid the burne of Liett upoun the southe syid of the brig of the samene, within the territorie of Hirsell Panneshauche, tuelff aikeris of land of the samene territorie of Hirsell Roundis and Braidspottis; all and haill the landis of Braidhauche, Dedriche and Leyis lyand on the southe syid of the burne of Leitte towarde the monasterie...the milne of Byirburnemilne [Fireburnmill] and the milne [mill] of Cauldstreme...[12]

Only one mill is mentioned above but, in 1651, in a charter under which James, Earl of Home grants land to his wife, Lady Jean Douglas, Countess of Home, reference is made to 'the mills of Cauldstreame which were demolished and destroyed in the time of war but are now rebuilt'.[13] Of these, 'Coldstream Mill' is referred to in *Second to None A History of Coldstream* in connection with a land dispute in 1566 which placed the mill 'a litill beneth the place of Hirsell on the eist syd of the watter, and the intak of the laid is tane in thair...'[14] This location ties in with the present position of the cauld but, in addition, the Armstrongs' map of 1771 shows a Spylaw Mill on the east bank of the Leet Water somewhere in the vicinity of Home Park, Coldstream, although to the west of it and at a lower level.[15]

Downstream and south-west of the cauld is a well-used

footbridge crossed by walkers using the footpath around The Hirsel's walled garden, past the 'Flodden tree' and along the south side of the house policies before dropping steeply down to the bridge. A field known as Dial Knowe is situated above the bridge to the west and is the site, at Grid Ref. NT830406, of a church dating from at least the 12th century and a cemetery that may have pre-dated it; there is also evidence of earlier occupation. In 1977, ploughing brought up gravestones of early Christian to early medieval types and, following a resistivity survey in 1978, excavation started in 1979, continuing into 1980. Pottery and wattle and daub from buildings provided evidence of Neolithic occupation and other timber and stone structures seemed to date from the 8th to 9th centuries.

Footbridge east of Dial Knowe field. 'Knowe' means 'knoll' or 'hillock'.

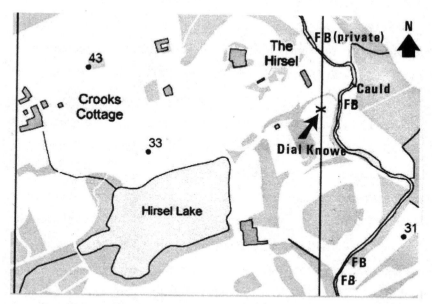

Map showing location of Dial Knowe field. 1 km. grid lines. Contains Ordnance Survey data © Crown copyright and database right 2012.

R. Cramp and C. Douglas-Home presented a comprehensive report on the discoveries to the Society of Antiquaries of Scotland in 1980. This included research on gifts and grants of land on The Hirsel estate as set out in the *Coldstream Cartulary* that provide evidence of the existence of the chapel (later a church) and cemetery. Details of coffins, grave markers and carvings were set out in the report, which also included maps and photographs. The earliest chapel was in existence by 1165-6.[16]

A perimeter wall of a cemetery was found south of the initial area, the final phase dating to the 13th century. Seven graves were discovered with three surviving adult skeletons. A burial platform was discovered between the enclosure and the north wall of the church and twenty-six burials were excavated with signs of three more. All the graves were stratified suggesting burial over a long period; unfortunately, the upper levels had been destroyed by ploughing. A small domestic building was found within the cemetery and excavation revealed the construction phases for the church.[17]

The Hirsel Museum has a display relating to the excavations including discoveries up to 1982 by which time over 260 graves had been discovered with different orientations and positions of the bodies. For example, in the 11th to 12th centuries, burials were in short cists or covered by slabs whereas in the 13th to 14th centuries the bodies were buried in dug graves with short, unmarked head or foot stones. The skeletons showed an appalling death toll of young children. There were 134 adults and 127 children and adolescents and, of the 127, 84 died under the age of 5 including 31 who seemed to be newborn or under one year.[18]

Many of the deaths would have been from infectious diseases such as enteritis, typhoid, smallpox, measles, influenza and whooping cough. Of the adults, few survived into old age, which would have started at 45 years in medieval times—perhaps six men or ten women were old. The rest died young, i.e. up to the age of 30 or into middle age, say 30 to 45 years. Disease and injury were prevalent—one man must have been a soldier as he had a healed sword-cut on his forehead and two fresh sword-cuts on his head. There were other examples of fractures of the skull, forearm and spine, all healed. Men were on average, 5ft. 6ins. in height and women, 5ft. 2ins. in height and all had teeth worn down by gritty flour, the flour having been ground by stone querns.[19]

The church was originally a single cell and expanded in five phases but, by the 13th and 14th centuries, there was evidence of domestic use although not in the original chancel of the church. Pottery and animal bones were found dating from the 13th to the 15th centuries and pottery use continued until the 16th century.[20] The church and cemetery seem to have gone out of use by the late 14th century and been superseded by domestic use until the 16th century.

The church and cemetery site at Dial Knowe, looking west from the footbridge over the Leet Water. There is nothing to see above ground but in medieval times it would have been a fairly prominent site on raised ground that has a particularly steep slope down to the Leet Water. The field is now in pasture with an enclosed area to the south planted with cattle fodder.

Even though it is used only by pedestrians, the footbridge below Dial Knowe field, like Dunglass Bridge, is supported by substantial rolled steel joists and is a good viewing platform with open views to the north and to the south. The water above and below the bridge is not overshadowed and, staring down into the currents, there are often shoals of small fish to be seen, looking black beneath the surface. The field on the left, the east bank, is one of a number on the estate where the Douglas and Hirsel Farms' fold of pedigree Douglas Highland cattle can often be seen grazing or lying around in the sun. The cattle come down to the Leet Water to drink on either

Looking downstream from the 'Dial Knowe bridge'.

side of the bridge, as evidenced by the cattle trods. There is a large sycamore in the middle of the field that provides shade for the cattle.

It must have been pollarded a long time ago and this may have caused the impressive burrs on its trunk, although they could have been caused by cattle grazing the side shoots, or by rubbing against them.

Sycamore with burrs; the bridge below Dial Knowe is in the distance.

South of the bridge, the Leet Water flows between the Dial Knowe field high on the west bank and the lower 'sycamore field' on the east bank before swinging south-east between the 'sycamore field' and land that now forms part of The Hirsel Golf Course. There is then a right-angled turn to the south-west along a straight stretch (see map on p. 117) with the golf course on the north-west side and a wooded area within which is a public footpath, on the south-east side.

At the right-angled turn, just north-east of map spot height 31 on p. 117, a footpath branches off south-east towards Coldstream, whereas the path following the course of the Leet Water continues south-west along the straight stretch, as mentioned above. The reason for mentioning the 'south-east path' is that, running alongside it, is a long stretch of the mill lade that would have served one or more of the mills mentioned on pp. 114-15. The lade will be mentioned again.

Meanwhile, the south-west straight stretch of the Leet Water drops down to where the golf course is on both banks and where there are two footbridges, the first for golfers only and the next for both golfers and walkers. The Hirsel Golf Club proudly describes itself as:

> the Augusta of The North. Breathlessly beautiful and pristine, it offers a stern challenge to the accomplished while being sympathetic to the beginner. Set in rolling woodland with thick shrubbery, fierce rough, water and other hazards in abundance. The current card reads 6024 yards, par 70. Founded in 1948. It is a course of strategic design with a fair margin for error. The fairways are generous, as are the greens, but getting from one to the other calls for more precision than power...[21]

The straight stretch, looking north-east towards the golfers' bridge.

The straight stretch, looking south-west towards the walkers' and golfers' bridge. The Leet Water runs through a 'manicured' landscape.

The public bridge used by walkers and golfers at Grid Ref. NT83054007 leads northwards towards the Homestead Visitor Centre. Downstream from the bridge, the Leet Water turns south and then south-east and continues in this direction, subject to meanders, until it passes under the Leet Bridge at Coldstream and leaves The Hirsel estate. Before this though, the Leet Water continues on its way through the golf course that includes belts and pockets of woodland as well as the neatly kept greens and fairways.

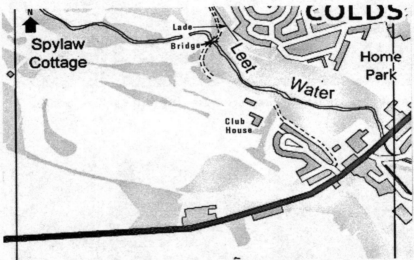

Map showing the route of the Leet water between the stone bridge (mentioned below and on pp. 125-6) and the A698 road at Coldstream. 1 km. grid lines. Contains Ordnance Survey data © Crown copyright and database right 2012.

At Grid Ref. NT83523988, the Leet Water passes under a stone bridge built by The Hirsel estate in 1893. Before that, the path (although it has now become a track) that passes over the bridge is the one described as the 'south-east path' on p.122, alongside which is a long stretch of the former mill lade. The lade is now silted up and would originally have been a deep and sharply defined channel as I almost found to my cost when standing in it to photograph one of the old arches beneath a minor crossing point. My boots were sticking and I realized that I must be standing on top of many feet of glutinous silt, as evidenced by the fact that the water level almost reached the top of the arch. Fortunately, I did not sink and I was able to admire the craftsmanship applied to the arch of what was only a small, unsurfaced, crossover, connecting fields to the 'south-east path'.

The beautifully carved and tightly fitting voussoirs of the crossing arch.

The 1893 single span bridge has some very fine stonework and it is interesting to speculate whether this came from quarries on the estate or elsewhere in Coldstream. There was a sandstone quarry on The Hirsel estate with a quarry house and an engine house near the site of the present Hirsel Golf Course Club-house, but the OS 1st edition 25 in. to 1 mile map of 1862 shows the quarry as flooded— perhaps it was later drained and was open for use 31 years later. Whoever built it and wherever the stone came from, the bridge has an attractive shallow arch, narrow pointing to the stonework and an inscription above the arch.

The stone bridge from the south-east.

Below the stone bridge, the Leet Water flows south-east for about a third of a mile until it passes under the A698 Leet Bridge carrying Coldstream High Street. The west side is wooded, separating the Leet Water from The Hirsel Golf Course Club-house, the Woodlands Park houses and Lees Farm. On the east side are the

126

woodlands below the Golf View houses, the Parkside houses and Home Park. Residential and other buildings do not intrude upon the green corridor, which continues all the way to the road bridge. The footpath on the east side is the continuation of the 'south-east path' mentioned before; this is now well above the Leet Water and separated from it by steeply sloping woodland. The 1862 OS map shows that there used to be a well down at the waterside near the 1893 bridge and another alongside the path near Home Park. The path finishes at the Court House car park in Coldstream.

The flood plain or haugh along this stretch of the Leet Water is quite marshy in places and can be overgrown in summer. Somewhere along here, a stone-age axe of indurated (hardened by heat or pressure) claystone, measuring almost three inches in length by one and three quarter inches across the cutting edge, was found in the bed of the Leet Water. It was in the collection of William Steele, F.S.A. Scot., who donated it in 1917 to the National Museum of Antiquities (housed with National Museums Scotland in Edinburgh).[22]

The origin of the name, 'Hirsel', according to Scots to English dictionaries, means a flock of sheep, a drove of cattle, an allotted area of pasturage to be grazed by a flock, a flock of anything, or a large number of anything. In John Thomson's *Atlas of Scotland*, 1832, the estate is shown as 'Herestale', a name not used on maps before or since. However, 'Herestale' was also used in the report of a case before the High Court of Justiciary in 1829 which determined that the Earl of Home's gamekeeper, James Craw, should be charged with murder or culpable homicide following the death of a poacher, John Guthrie, who tripped a wire trigger of a loaded spring-gun.[23]

May Williamson noted other spellings used in old documents, Herishill in 1165 and c. 1200, Herisehill in c. 1200, Hereshille in 1200 and c. 1320, Hershill in 1246, Hersil in 1269, Hershale in 1292 and Hirsale in c. 1443.[24]

This stretch of the Leet Water through The Hirsel estate finishes at Leet Bridge, at the west end of Coldstream. It has brought me down into the outskirts of Coldstream and, again, has been quite different from what has gone before, just as all the previous stretches have had their own distinguishing characters. This time, there has been the experience of travelling through magnificent woodland with many large native and exotic trees planted by the Earls of Home, mainly during the 19th century. There has been well-maintained parkland, grazing and arable land as well as the historic house, the estate buildings and cottages, the golf course and the visitors' centre. There is a great deal of history and prehistory, even if some of it is not visible above ground such as the medieval church and cemetery at Dial Knowe or the fort on Hirsel Law. I found Hirsel Law to be an unexpected feature, hidden from below because of the tree-covered slopes even though the summit is the highest point on the estate with impressive views to the south and west.

6

Leet Bridge to Tweed

On the north side of the Leet Bridge is one of 392 gauging stations throughout Scotland, monitored by the Scottish Environment Protection Agency (SEPA). Information on water levels and flows is collected automatically and transferred from the data management system to the website once every hour. SEPA has a statutory responsibility to gather information and to act upon it—for example, under the Water Framework Directive 2000, the approach to water management includes 'the licensing of water abstraction, the control of diffuse pollution and the consideration of flow regimes in environmental standards'. Flood management and a climate change remit are other reasons for having the gauging stations.

The information gathered from the gauging station on the Leet Water at Grid Ref. NT83983965 is published online (as is information from all 392 stations) because SEPA recognises that it can be useful to others. Records started in 1986. The station has a trapezoidal flume for measuring water flow and it also measures the water level. In addition to current measurements, the website gives highest, lowest and average levels on record and other useful data. The highest level on record was 3.976 m. at 14.45 on 22nd October

Looking north from the Leet Bridge, Coldstream showing the trapezoidal flume that is part of the SEPA gauging station.

2002.[1] At the top of the wall on the right hand side of the photograph, there is a high water indicator that can be seen from the bridge showing water levels from 3.0 m. to 3.5 m.

The Leet Bridge at Coldstream at Grid Ref. NT83973959, which carries the A698 road from Berwick to Kelso, is a mid 20th century reinforced concrete replacement for an earlier stone bridge. In the first photograph overleaf, the horizontal parapets of the old bridge can be seen beyond the Lees Mill buildings on the right behind the trees and beyond the sloping approach parapets on both sides of the road. The road was 'metalled' but not surfaced in tarmacadam and would have been either unpleasantly muddy or dry and dusty.

19th century view looking towards the Leet Bridge and High Street.
Photograph by permission of Dorothy Jenkins.

21st century view; Lees Mill has gone; the turning on the right goes down
to the Irish Bridge, the converted Lees stables, modern housing and Lees
Haugh.

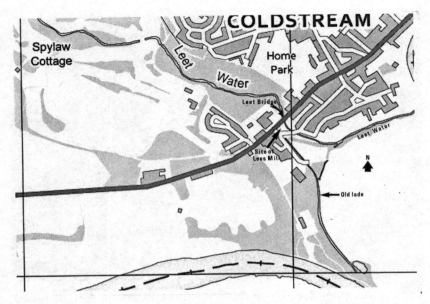

Map showing area of the Leet Bridge at Coldstream. 1 km. grid lines. The Irish Bridge is south-east of Leet Bridge, on the grid line. Contains Ordnance Survey data © Crown copyright and database right 2012.

The photographs on p. 131 show that the view has changed since the 19th but not as much as might be expected. The bridge itself has changed, Lees Mill has gone, the road has been surfaced and 'dinosaur' street lamps are dominant but the scene is still recognisable due to the survival of most of the Victorian and earlier buildings fronting the High Street. The High Street is named as such on the OS 1st edition map of 1862 but, before that, it was known as the Edinburgh-Newcastle-London road.

Blackadder shows the Leet Bridge in 1797 but the Armstrong map, in 1771, shows that the main road is still from Market Square to the ford across the Leet Water. In 1771, the Leet Bridge has been built but it does not yet connect with the High Street (see maps following).[2]

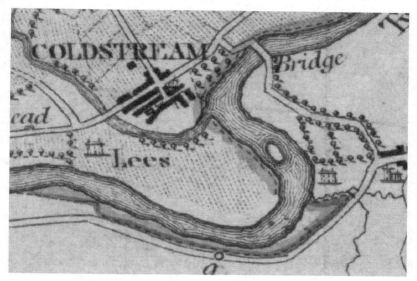

Extract from John Blackadder's map of 1797 showing the small village of Coldstream with Leet Bridge and Coldstream Bridge. Reproduced by permission of the Trustees of the National Library of Scotland.

Extract from the earlier Armstrongs' map of 1771, only four years after Coldstream Bridge was opened. The Leet Bridge, upstream from the ford, is unconnected to the east. Reproduced by permission of the Trustees of the National Library of Scotland.

133

However, William Walker, writing in 1954, says that the bridge was built by Dr. James Pringle of The Lees, the son of Pringle of Torsonce and Rachel Marjoribanks and that he also built the mansion house.[3] Dr. Pringle died in 1769, unmarried and left the Lees estate to his cousin, Edward Marjoribanks, a wine merchant in Bordeaux, who died in 1815.[4] So, the Leet Bridge could have been built in the 1760s and the High Street extended to meet it between 1771 and 1797.

Edward's son, Sir John Marjoribanks, 1st Baronet, became MP for the County of Berwick and Lord Provost of Edinburgh; he died in 1833. Sir John's younger son, Charles Marjoribanks was in the civil service of the East India Company; he succeeded his father as MP for Berwickshire and sat as a Liberal until his own death in the same year, 1833. The monument at the east end of Coldstream commemorates his election and achievements after the first Reform Act of 1832. Charles's nephew, the second Sir John Marjoribanks is remembered by the memorial in front of Coldstream Parish Church that recognises his efforts in bringing water to the town in 1852.[5]

Walker also says (in 1954) that the stone bridge had been 'lately demolished, to be succeeded by the present metal and cement construction'.[6] Before the Leet Bridge was built and before Smeaton's Coldstream Bridge was built across the River Tweed between 1763 and 1767, access to Coldstream from the south by ferry or ford across the Tweed and from the west by ford or stepping stones across the Leet Water would have been difficult when water levels were high.

In 1954, The Lees was owned by Major John and Captain L. Scott Briggs and was described by Walker as 'externally, a work of great beauty, of disciplined architectural taste, and of craftsmanship of the first order...it is, in its western frontage, a masterpiece of restraint and balance of its parts...'[7] Walker also referred to its having 'taken the place of the older family house adjoining the present stabling at its southern end'.[8] The second house was of two-storey and basement construction with a semi-circular bow front with classical columns in the centre of the west elevation.

The estate came into the ownership of a branch of the Home family but the mansion fell into disrepair during the 20th century, and most of it had to be demolished. Fortunately, Mr. Andrew Douglas-Home, the present owner, has carried out a sympathetic reconstruction resulting in a third house built on a smaller scale but in vernacular style; an inspired feature is the extension of the semi-circular bow to form a complete rotunda with conical roof.

Looking south from Leet Bridge to the Irish Bridge, Coldstream.

Below the Leet Bridge, the Leet Water turns south-east to flow under the Irish Bridge before turning north-east. Lees Mill is not on Crawford's map of 1843 but it is shown on the OS 1st Edition 25 inches to the mile map of 1862. It was a corn mill fronting Kelso Road operated by a water wheel that took water from a lade; the intake for the lade was on the River Tweed, east of The Lees temple.

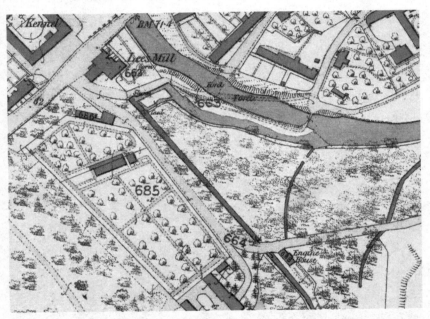

Extract from OS 25 inch to 1 mile, 1st Edition, Berwick Sheet XXIX.9, 1862 showing Lees Mill, the lade, the sluices, the engine house and inflow and outfall for The Lees. Reproduced by permission of the Trustees of the National Library of Scotland.

The layout on the map looks rather complicated but, in essence, the lade supplied the water for the headrace to power the wheel following which the water was discharged into a tailrace that flowed into the Leet Water next to the spit of land marked on the map

136

with the parcel number 663. The sluice and caul (sic) were both part of the system.

There was an engine house (now a private house) that pumped water from the Leet Water up to The Lees.[9] The intake channel can be seen on the map coming up from the Leet Water and under the track; the channel to the east must have been an outfall from The Lees. The mill was demolished in the 20th century and part of the site is now a small car park with the remainder of the land laid out with grass and trees alongside the Leet Water.

The mid 20th century reinforced concrete Leet Bridge at Coldstream.

In 1862, there was still a connection between Kelso Road and Duke Street and Leet Street by way of two fords that crossed over to the spit of land separating the Leet Water from the outfall from Lees

Mill. There was also a footbridge opposite Leet Street and a modern replacement is still there. The mill lade survives for all of its original length but the outfalls from the mill with the sluice and the caul (sic), have been filled in. The fords have been replaced by the 'Irish Bridge'. In civil engineering terms, an Irish Bridge is an improved ford designed to withstand the effects of water in times of periodic flooding by allowing the flood water to flow over the top of it and not just beneath it. In dry periods, it looks like a normal bridge with pavements and railings but the lower structure, at the same level as the land on either side of it, has a cheaper construction cost.

The low level Irish Bridge trapping debris as flood-waters rise.

Although all traces of Lees Mill seem to have disappeared as a result of the construction of the new bridge and the car park, there is still a section of old wall projecting at right angles to the concrete retaining wall of the bridge approach. It looks as though it could have been part of the retaining wall that once separated the north-east side of the mill building and access paths from the lower area. It is now a retaining wall of the car park. The 1862 map on p. 136 shows the line of the wall and the lower area that has a footpath running through it.

The old wall has a small hollowed out recess containing a lead spout with a notice above it saying 'Drinking Water'—a quaint feature that no longer appears to serve its purpose, at least not when I was there.

There have been many changes to the bed and banks of the Leet Water since the closure of the mill as a result of the infilling of the outfalls, the consequent disappearance of the 'spit' and the restructuring of the land on either side to accommodate the road now linking the ends of Duke Street and Leet Street, across to Kelso Road. On the far bank of the Leet Water opposite Duke Street, there are vestiges of rubble walling that may have been part of the south-east angle of the lower mill area, or perhaps part of the 'sluices-caul-outfall-spit-ford' constructions shown on the 1862 map. But, this is just conjecture.

A late 19th century or very early 20th century view of the Lees Mill/Leet Bridge area. Image reproduced by permission of Dorothy Jenkins.

A 21st century view. The cottages are still there, the mill and outfalls have gone and the arched bridge and fords have modern replacements.

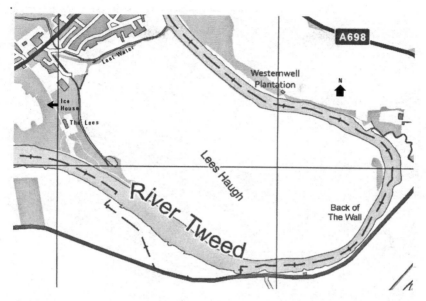

Modern map showing the Leet Water, The Lees, the ice-house, Lees Haugh and the River Tweed, Coldstream. 1 km. grid lines. Contains Ordnance Survey data © Crown copyright and database right 2012.

Having mentioned the ice-house at The Hirsel, it is worth going a little bit off course to look at the one at The Lees on the

south-west side of the drive, at Grid Ref. NT83913932 (see right). Unlike The Hirsel ice house (now just a depression in the ground) which had a thatched roof and timber walls, this one at The Lees is of stone construction covered with earth and is in good condition. It may only be viewed from the outside.

141

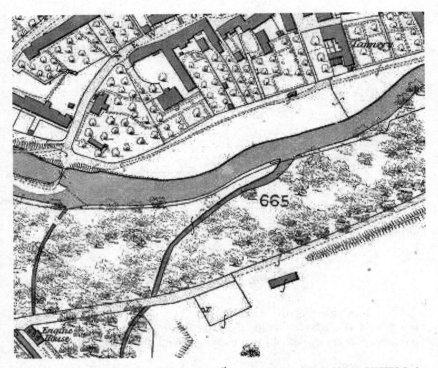

Extract from OS 25 inch to 1 mile, 1ˢᵗ Edition, Berwick Sheet XXIX.9, in 1862, showing the footbridge, the engine house and the intake and outfall channels to and from The Lees. Note the former tannery behind the wall to the north of the Leet Water. This was to the west of the brewery. Reproduced by permission of the Trustees of the National Library of Scotland.

Below the footbridge (downstream from the Irish Bridge), the Leet Water runs alongside the footpath and Leet Green on the north bank and the wooded area backing on to Lees Haugh on the south bank. It is still possible to see traces of the mouth of the outfall from The Lees which, in 1862, was north of the land parcel number 665 on the above map. There is also some surviving stonework that must have defined and strengthened the banks at this point. Much of the channel was infilled a long time ago, but a good section can be seen next to the stone bridge carrying the track to Lees Haugh, north-east of the former engine house.

The Leet Water and its banks, between Leet Bridge and the River Tweed could be the place to see an otter, depending upon the

time of day, the absence of people and the invisibility of the observer. However, perhaps the hide on the south side of The Hirsel lake would provide more opportunities. The European otter *Lutra lutra*, is native to the River Tweed and its tributaries, including the Leet Water. Over the years, the otter population in the United Kingdom suffered from persecution, loss of habitat and the use of insecticides

'Otter' by Emily-Ieva Chessell, aged 5, 2008

until, at one time, it had diminished to such an extent that strong concentrations were only to be found in Scotland, particularly the north and west and parts of the Borders, as well as parts of Wales and Ireland. Fortunately, there has been a recovery in numbers and, due to improvements in water quality and, consequently, more sustainable fish populations in rivers, otters are now to be found throughout the United Kingdom.[10]

An otter usually lives for three or four years, but this can be longer and it inhabits a 'home range' of up to 12 miles or more of river bank, feeding mainly on a variety of fish species but also small mammals and birds, depending upon availability at the time. In Scotland, the otter is protected under The Conservation (Natural Habitats, etc.) Amendment (Scotland) Regulations 1994, enhanced by regulations in 2007 which make it illegal to 'deliberately or recklessly kill, injure or take an otter; deliberately or recklessly disturb or harass an otter; damage, destroy or obstruct access to a breeding site or resting place of an otter'. The presence of otters in the River Tweed catchment is a contributory reason for the catchment's selection as a Special Area of Conservation (SAC) under Article 3 of the European Commission's Habitat Directive. The River Tweed SAC is part of a European network of high-quality conservation sites that will make a significant contribution to conserving the 189 habitat types and 788 species (the otter is one) identified in Annexes I and II of the Directive (as amended).

On the far side of Leet Green on the north-west side of the Leet Water, from the end of Leet Street to Tweed Green, runs the footpath known as Penitent's Walk. It runs along the side of the wall that can be seen on the 1862 map on p. 142 and on the map on p. 154. Penitent's (only one?—there must have been more) Walk connects with a footpath at the back of, and above Tweed Green, that leads to Nuns Walk—the latter becomes a high-level, exposed walk above the River Tweed before it reaches the observation area near the monument to Charles Marjoribanks on the A698 road.

N

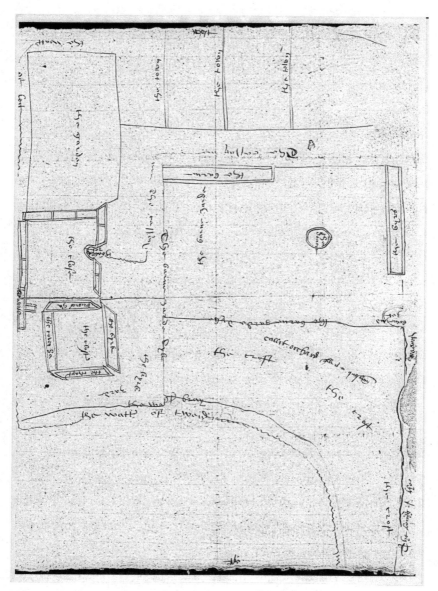

Plan of St. Mary's Abbey (Coldstream Priory) lands and buildings, Coldstream, 1589. NRS RHP49993 Reproduced by permission of the National Records of Scotland.

Penitent's Walk and Nuns Walk are names that evoke the former Coldstream Priory that once occupied a large area of land on the north side of the Leet Water at this point although it is not known whether these are original names or whether they arose later on. Coldstream Priory was home to a Cistercian Order of nuns and was the dominant influence in Coldstream from its foundation in 1165/6 until its dissolution in 1587. Unfortunately, there are no standing remains of the priory; robbed out stonework may have been incorporated into buildings and boundary walls in Coldstream but the site was demitted to Sir John Hamilton of Trabrown in 1621 and used as a quarry, so the stonework may have been dispersed far and wide.[11]

The priory was a powerful landowner in Coldstream and for a considerable distance round about and the farms, mills and orchards would have yielded a good financial return. Wool was a particularly valuable product for export until such time as the port of Berwick upon Tweed ceased to be in Scottish hands. Five members of the Hoppringle family were prioresses of Coldstream and it was Isabella Hoppringle who was prioress at the time of the battle of Flodden in 1513 and arranged for the slain Scottish nobility to be brought back for burial in consecrated ground at Tweed Green. The priory was situated close to the ford across the River Tweed near the mouth of the Leet Water, across which came invading Scottish and English armies that were often billeted in Coldstream, perhaps for weeks, waiting for the water level to drop.

The main buildings of the priory fronted the Leet Water across the grass area known as Leet Green. If the 1589 plan on p. 145 is turned sideways with ⬆ to the top, the 'watter of leet' bends round from left to right along the bottom of the page into the 'watter of tweed' on the right hand side. Because of the feint, archaic script on the old document, it is difficult to make out some of the details of the plan. Facing the Leet Water (from the left) is the walled, priory garden. Next to it is the close, which is a courtyard surrounded by buildings, with a gatehouse on the north side. These were probably domestic, working buildings for the priory. Then comes the cloister with a church (kyrke) on the north side, the chapter house on the east side, the refectory on the south side and the prioress's house on the west side. The graveyard is to the east overlooking the River Tweed. Barns, yards, orchards and gardens lie to the north.[12]

The priory must have encompassed the sites of the present Duke Street, Leet Street, Market Square and Tweed Road and much of the surrounding land but any archaeological investigation would be very difficult because of the present site coverage. There have been occasional finds in the past such as fragments of stone now placed in Coldstream Museum. Also, a small pack-horse bridge was discovered at Grid Ref. NT84173966, described in 1868 as 'about 6 ft. wide with an arch of $2\frac{1}{2}$ ft. high and side walls 5 ft. apart and 5 ft. high. The road which crossed the bridge consisted of a thin crust of cinders and gravel, with some broken stones and fragments of pottery'.[13]

The bridge was in the garden of James Briggs near Duke Street, $4\frac{1}{2}$ ft. below the surface and was 'on a direct line between the convent (sic) and the ford over the Leet'. It may therefore have been on the line of the causeway that approached from the north and gave access to the priory at the gatehouse. In 1966, it was said that the remains of the bridge were still there, underground.[14]

The priory was sited on higher ground above Leet Green and Tweed Green as evidenced by the present houses and gardens behind and well above Penitent's Walk and the house and garden at Abbey House, which overlooks Tweed Green. This was necessary because Leet Green and Tweed Green are flooded perhaps once or even twice a year.

Himalayan Balsam on the east bank of the Leet Water near its mouth.

In the photograph above, the Leet Water has overflowed on to Leet Green to the left of a line of Himalayan balsam, *Impatiens glandulifera*. This plant has an attractive flower, being a relative of the busy lizzie, but it is a major weed problem on river banks and waste ground. It was introduced to the UK in 1839 since when it has spread rapidly; it also grows fast to well over head-height, forming huge clumps that quickly smother native vegetation (see above).

Himalayan balsam is not the only invasive plant that causes problems. There are also giant hogweed (*Heracleum mantegazzianum*), Japanese knotweed (*Fallopia japonica*) and giant knotweed (*Fallopia sachalinensis*). These species were introduced into Britain in the 19th century as exotic plants for garden collections. As garden escapees into the natural environment, river systems enabled them to reproduce rapidly by carrying their seeds and rhizomes downstream. In the Borders, the River Tweed and its tributaries (including parts of the Leet water) were infested by the plants and, by the early 1980s, it was realized that efforts to control their spread by cutting and strimming were ineffectual. Handling giant hogweed causes blistering and burns to the skin.

Giant hogweed and Japanese knotweed can grow in a wide range of soil conditions, are shade tolerant species and form dense canopies above the height of native species that cannot compete with them. Giant hogweed can also cause erosion of river banks because when an individual plant dies, its roots leave large holes in soil which has no strength or stability having lost the binding effect of native plants. Large sections of bank can collapse, smothering the gravel habitats of fish and invertebrate populations; also, the collapse can alter the water surface/volume ratios, causing temperature spikes that can kill fish.

In 2002, the Tweed Invasives Project was set up, led by the Tweed Forum, the membership of which comprised organizations on both sides of the river and on both sides of the border.[15] The Tweed

149

Forum was established in 1991 to 'promote the wise and sustainable use of the Tweed and its tributaries through holistic and integrated management and planning'. In the late 1990s, the establishment of the Tweed Rivers Heritage Project in partnership with the Tweed Forum's thirty or so members, enabled the Tweed Invasives Project to become one of the fifty constituent projects of the overall Tweed Rivers Heritage Project. The Tweed Invasives Project concentrated on tackling the problems of giant hogweed and Japanese knotweed with initial funding from various sources to cover an initial three year period with possible extensions thereafter. The project involved many organizations, landowners, farmers and volunteers in an annual programme of spraying along the whole length of the river and along parts of the tributaries.

Giant hogweed. Photograph reproduced by permission of Coldstream & District Angling Association.

Experience has taught the Tweed Forum that spraying has to be carried out at the right time. Giant hogweed has staggered germination times for both seedlings and over wintering plants from February until the end of July depending upon soil conditions, aspect and altitude and it is important to delay spraying in order to achieve the best results and to avoid having to carry out repeat spraying in the same year.

Japanese knotweed is far more difficult to eradicate than giant hogweed as it is highly resistant to spraying, cutting, or grazing by animals. It can start to grow in March with significant growth in May. Digging out the plants and their rhizomes is effective but is labour-intensive. Constant spraying of new growth, repeated three or four times a year to weaken and finally destroy the plants seems to be the most practical solution, but this involves a great deal of monitoring. Spraying the young plants is the most effective method, before the plants have grown to a height of 8 to 12 feet.

Himalayan balsam is a difficult plant to eradicate by spraying because it grows amongst native plants. The Tweed Forum set up a pilot study and found that the only way to control and eradicate the plant was by hand pulling, including the roots. Spraying was not an option because balsam is interspersed amongst native plants and, unlike the large and dense hogweed and knotweed, cannot be isolated from them. It was therefore necessary to employ contractors to supplement the hard work that fell upon landowners and volunteers. The study was continued in 2006 with follow-up site monitoring and control work. Coldstream & District Angling Association is one of the volunteer organizations that have been participating in the Tweed

Invasives Project by chemical spraying of giant hogweed every year along (1) the steep slopes below Nuns' Walk, (2) the bunds at Leet Haugh, (3) between Cornhill on Tweed and the river, (4) the banks and field margins west of The Lees, (5) the banks of the Leet Water from its junction with the Tweed up to Leet Bridge and beyond.

Results suggest that great progress has been made in controlling all these invasive species but it is an ongoing project and it will be some time before any claims can be made regarding complete eradication.

I have dwelt at some length on dealing with invasive plant species but I believe that this is with good reason as it is a serious problem that has to be dealt with, including the eradication of plants along the banks of the Leet Water. The Wildlife and Countryside Act 1981 amended by the Wildlife and Natural Environment (Scotland) Act 2011 aims to prevent the release and spread of non-native animals and plants, ensure a rapid response to new populations and ensure effective control and eradication. The inclusion of non-native animals reflects, for example, the concern regarding predators that can affect native fish stocks and their environment.

Native predators such as the otter, kingfisher and heron are accepted, as the 'damage' they do is insufficient to affect the overall balance of the environment. However, alien species that have already arrived or may arrive soon are a serious threat to the environment. Even the goosander with its serated saw bill (for the easy catching of fish) is alien to Britain (even though, since its arrival in the 19th century, it is now becoming native) and is a threat to salmon smolts and large parr with consequent economic damage to fishing. The

Tweed Foundation has produced posters of eight unwanted species of crab, crayfish, fish and microscopic organisms that could oust native species, cause disease or even, as with the American or signal crayfish *Pacifastacus leniusculus*, cause damage by undermining the banks, making them dangerous for farm animals.

Coldstream & District Angling Association has also been involved in other work on the Tweed and its tributaries, including the Leet Water, with the Tweed Forum and the Tweed Trout and Grayling Initiative (TTGI) to measure fish levels by means of electro-fishing, a process that temporarily stuns the fish without harming them in order to allow biologists to measure them and take scale samples for ageing. The TTGI was set up with European money but is now largely funded by angling associations to create self-sustaining management of the wild trout and grayling fisheries within the Tweed system.

On previous pages, I have mentioned legislation, statutory and other bodies and the many projects and initiatives at local, national and European level that help to protect and enhance the environment of the Tweed catchment. It is also worth mentioning the Solway Tweed River Basin Management Plan prepared by SEPA for Scotland and the Environment Agency for England. The plan is a requirement of the European Union's Water Framework Directive and sets a framework for enhancing the water environment from 2009 to 2015 with some commitments possibly extending to 2021 or 2027. For the Tweed, the Tweed Forum Executive Committee and other organizations from Scotland and England, meet as the Tweed Area Advisory Group to progress the Tweed Area Management Plan.[16]

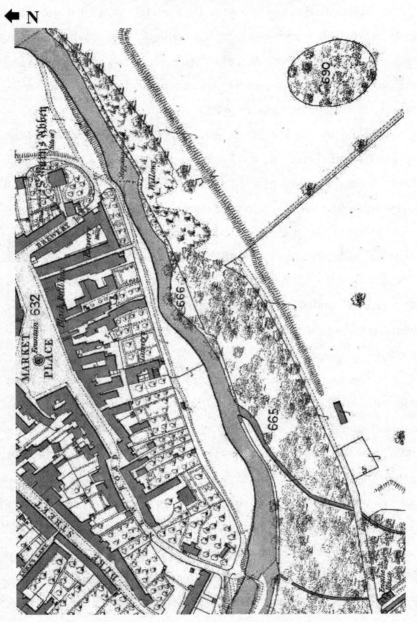

Extract from OS 25 inch to 1 mile, 1ˢᵗ Edition, Berwick Sheet XXIX.9, 1862, showing the lower reach of the Leet Water. Reproduced by permission of the Trustees of the National Library of Scotland.

LEET BRIDGE TO TWEED

From opposite the end of Abbey Road (named on the 1862 OS map as Brewery Lane because of the brewery that was there well into the 20th century) to its confluence with the River Tweed, the Leet Water flows between Tweed Green on its north bank and woodland fronting Lees Haugh, on its south bank. Behind the woodland, can be seen one of the bunds or earth dykes built for Sir James Marjoribanks in about 1820 by Napoleonic prisoners of war. The bunds with their inbuilt sluices control water that from time to time floods Lees Haugh, depositing silt that adds to the fertility of the land.

Leet Water looking upstream near the site of the former stepping stones.

Across from the end of Brewery Lane, the 1862 map shows some stepping-stones leading across the Leet Water to the area marked 'Willows'. The crossing is no longer in use and although it is tempting to think that the many parallel lines of stones across the Leet Water in the photograph above may be relics of the crossing, the stones may just be natural deposits due to the flow of water. Immediately upstream at this point, the north bank is reinforced by gabions comprising stone-filled, welded-mesh cages. They are linked together, making for quick construction and to allow plants to establish themselves between the stones and through the mesh. The gabion wall can be seen as the steep-sided bank beyond the tree on the right hand side, looking upstream.

Earlier on, there was a brief mention of some of the birds to be seen along the course of the Leet Water but there was no attempt to give a comprehensive listing. As the Leet Water nears the Tweed, there is a chance to see not only those waterside birds most associated with small watercourses, such as kingfishers and dippers, but also others that are at home on larger, faster-flowing rivers. There is a chance to see the grey wagtail *Motacilla cinerea* with its grey upper parts and lemon-yellow under parts that can be seen along farmyards and small rivers in winter and searching for insects along fast-flowing rivers in summer. In summer, it may be possible to see a much more rare and endangered member of the same family, the yellow wagtail *Motacilla flava*, a small yellow and green bird that migrates to Africa in winter.

Some birds more commonly associated with coastal locations have also moved inland in recent years and so there is a chance to see a perching, black cormorant *Phalacrocorax carbo* spreading its wings out to dry or the black oystercatcher *Haematopus ostralegus* with its long orange-red bill and reddish-pink legs. The former is a fish-eater and can cause problems for anglers; the latter eats mussels and cockles on the coast but is content with worms, inland.

Looking towards the mouth of the Leet Water where it meets the River Tweed.

LEET WATER FROM SOURCE TO TWEED

Having gradually descended thirteen or more miles, the Leet Water finally meets the River Tweed (Grid Ref. NT84493965) at the historic spot mentioned on p. 146 where the ford used to cross the River Tweed between England and Scotland and where, on Tweed Green, the bodies of the fallen Scots nobility probably still lie. The Leet Water flows into the Tweed almost at a right angle rather than turning down stream as does the River Teviot where it flows into the Tweed at Kelso. At first I thought that this was unusual and that the Leet Water was maintaining to the end, the waywardness and unconventional directions of flow that had started at its source. However, I realized that many of the tributaries of the Tweed entered the river more or less at ninety degrees, even if their general direction, unlike the Leet Water, goes with the flow of the receiving river. The mouth of the Leet Water shown in the photograph on p. 157, taken in summer, shows a very low water level whereas the photograph on p. 159, again taken in summer, shows a fairly high water level.

This last stretch of the Leet Water from Leet Bridge to the mouth has been very short, but no less interesting because of it. It has been dominated by the proximity and history of the sites of Lees Mill and Coldstream Priory and the presence of The Lees estate on one side and the edge of the built up area of Coldstream on the other. I finished this section in late spring (although some photographs were taken at other times), twelve months after I started my journey at the source and I was conscious of coming full circle with a repeat performance of the lush new growth of plants. On this last stretch, I was aware that, despite the proximity of the town, the woodland and tree margins extended right along the south bank as far as the mouth.

The mouth of the Leet Water as it enters the River Tweed from the right with Lees Haugh behind.

There were flourishing wild plants and flowers in the understorey and in the long grass beyond the trees next to Lees Haugh and I particularly noticed the swathes of ramsons *Allium ursinum* with their white flowers, long green leaves and strong garlic smell. Standing apart from these in the grass was garlic mustard *Alliaria petiolata* with its four-petalled white flowers clustered at the tips of the stems and quite large triangular leaves that, when crushed, also smell of garlic. Also, there was the white dead-nettle *Lamium album*; it resembles the common nettle but does not have stinging hairs and its young leaves, flowers and roots have culinary and medicinal uses.

This brings me to the end of my journey and one that I finish with a great deal of regret, having enjoyed the variety of scenery and discovered such a surprising amount of history and information along the way. There have been so many contrasts—arable land, pasture, woodland and marshland on farms and landed estates. The Leet Water is slow running in places, fast flowing in others, with straight sections and meandering ones, flowing under old bridges and new bridges, below high cliffs and through fords, next to embankments and past lades. It is a magnet for wildlife above the waterline and a haven for acquatic species below and is a valuable spawning ground.

The Leet Water is small, modest and a hidden delight—a gem that deserves to be known beyond Whitsome, Swinton and Coldstream, but perhaps we would rather keep it a secret.

Appendix

I have mentioned some plants throughout the book but, for a fuller picture, it may be helpful to refer readers to the relevant paragraphs from Michael Braithwaite's *Botanical Tour of Berwickshire* written in his capacity as a Vice-county Recorder for the Botanical Society of the British Isles. The paragraphs are reproduced here with the kind permission of the author.

NT83

The Leet Water is a wildlife corridor across the heart of the agricultural land of the Merse with grassland, wetland and fragmentary woodland. This corridor continues through to its junction with the Tweed. Below The Hirsel Clustered Dock *Rumex conglomeratus* occurs at the river margin near Common Club-rush *Schoenoplectus lacustris*, while a haugh area supports Meadow Fescue *Festuca pratensis* and the hybrid grass *X Festulolium loliaceum* with a little Agrimony *Agrimonia eupatoria*. The woodland has False-brome *Brachypodium sylvaticum* and Hairy St John's-wort *Hypericum hirsutum* and a little Wall Lettuce *Mycelis muralis*. While this is a natural habitat for the Wall Lettuce, the plants are probably just outliers of the large populations on walls in Coldstream and at The Hirsel and it is perhaps best considered as an introduction, as elsewhere in Berwickshire.

NT84

Part of The Merse is drained by the Leet Water, which cuts across the general lie of the land and meanders for several kilometres across haughs between grassy banks. There its flora has fared better, though the aquatic flora has largely been lost to eutrophication.

The wooded policies at The Hirsel contain many old trees, in some places with a shrubby understory and open glades. These have allowed Cowslip *Primula veris* to prosper with a double-flowered variety of Meadow Saxifrage *Saxifraga granulata*, doubtless naturalised from an introduction. Wall Lettuce *Mycelis muralis* is widespread and may be an accidental introduction that has spread. The woods at a distance from the house are managed in a way that preserves some more natural features. Notable relict species are Common Wintergreen *Pyrola minor* and Oak Fern *Gymnocarpion dryopteris*, but Twayblade *Listera ovata* has not been seen since 1985. Both Silver Birch *Betula pendula* and Downy Birch *B. pubescens* are frequent and this is perhaps the one area in Berwickshire where Silver Birch might have a true native population. Elsewhere it is naturalised from plantings and now much planted, almost to the exclusion of Downy Birch.

LEET WATER FROM SOURCE TO TWEED

The Leet Water is notable as a wildlife corridor across the heart of the agricultural land of The Merse with grassland, wetland and fragmentary woodlands. At The Hirsel Marsh Ragwort *Senecio aquaticus*, with the hybrid Ragwort *S. x ostenfeldii*, and Clustered Dock *Rumex conglomeratus* occur in the cattle-plodged river margins while the haugh fields support Meadow Fescue *Festuca pratensis* and the hybrid grass *X Festulolium loliaceum* with Lady's-mantle *Alchemilla* species. Throughout the corridor the banksides have much False-brome *Brachypodium sylvaticum* with frequent Hairy St John's-wort *Hypericum hirsutum* and a little Agrimony *Agrimonia eupatoria*. In Rough Haugh and Wylie Cleugh there are very extensive stands of the robust sedge *Carex riparia* with a little of the rather similar *C. acuta* and *C. otrubae*. There are a few modest colonies of Common Club-rush *Schoenoplectus lacustris* in the Leet itself or at its banks.

There are few ponds. Much the largest is Hirsel Lake. This has a modest aquatic flora where rigid Hornwort *Ceratophyllum demersum* and Lesser Pondweed *Potamogeton pusillus* have now been joined by Least Duckweed *Lemna minuta*. At the margin there is much Bittersweet *Solanum dulcamara* and a little Bladder Sedge *Carex vesicaria*, while Skullcap *Scutellaria galericulata* was recorded in 1997 in a reed bed, now the only colony known in Berwickshire if indeed it is still present. A pond at Morningbank which seems to be a remnant of a former oxbow of the Leet Water has a strong colony of Grey Club-rush *Schoenoplectus tabernaemontani*, the only Berwickshire station.

Notes

CHAPTER 1 – Setting the Scene

1. Ed. Frances H. Groome, *Ordnance Gazetteer of Scotland: A Survey of Scottish Topography, Statistical, Biographical, and Historical*, Volume IV, Thomas C. Jack, Grange Publishing Works, Edinburgh, London, Glasgow, Aberdeen, 1885, p. 480

2. Scottish Environmental Protection Agency (SEPA), Indicative River & Coastal Flood Map, 2010, accessed online at http://go.mappoint.net/sepa/

3. See dictionary definitions for 'leet' or 'leat' and, for a more in-depth study, see Williamson, May G., *The Non-Celtic Place-Names of the Scottish Border Counties*, unpublished PhD thesis, University of Edinburgh, 1942, (www.spns.org.uk/MayWilliamsonComplete.pdf, p. 67)

4. (i) Plan of St. Mary's Abbey lands and buildings, Coldstream, Berwickshire, 1589, Reference RHP49993, Repository Code 234, The National Archives of Scotland (ii) Sharpe, Peter, fl. 1785-1818, Plan of Coldstream, Earl of Haddington's Property, [ca. 1818], Shelfmark EMS.S.371, National Library of Scotland (iii) Blackadder, John, fl. 1793-1830, map of Berwickshire, 1797, Shelfmark EMS.s.46, National Library of Scotland (iv) Crawford, William, 1793-ca.1845; Brooke, William, fl. 1835-47, North-east sheet of Map embracing extensive portions of the Counties of Roxburgh, Berwick, Selkirk & Midlothian and Part of Northumberland, Imprint, W. Forrester: Edinburgh, [1843], Shelfmark: Newman 1097, National Library of Scotland

5. Williamson, May G., *The Non-Celtic Place-Names of the Scottish Border Counties* p. 66

6. ibid., p. 66, pp. 67-8

7. For information on traditional Coldstream buildings, see Chessell, Antony, *Coldstream Building Snippets 'Cans, Quoins and Coursers'*, Lulu Publishing, 2010

8. A useful readable guide to local geology is *East Lothian and the Borders A Landscape fashioned by Geology*, Scottish Natural Heritage and British Geological Survey, 1997

9. For a good description of drumlins, see Everest, Jeremy; Bradwell, Tom; Colledge, Nick, *Subglacial Landforms of the Tweed Palaeo-Ice Stream* (Scottish Landform Example No. 35), British Geological Survey, Edinburgh, 2005

10. *'Old' Statistical Account of Scotland, 1791-1799*, Number XXXVI. United Parishes of Swinton and Simprin (Presbytery of Chirnside, Synod of Merse and Tiviotdale, County of Berwick) *By the Rev.* Mr. George Cupples, drawn up by Sir John Sinclair, printed by William Creech, Edinburgh, p. 322 ff.; Number XIX, United

Parishes of Whitsome and Hilton (County of Berwick, Synod of Merse and Teviot-Dale and Presbytery of Churnside) *By the Rev.* Mr George Cupples, *Minister of Swinton,* p. 348 ff.; Number LV, Parish of Coldstream (County of Berwick) *By* James Bell, D.D, p. 410 ff.

'New' Statistical Account of Scotland, 1834-45, Vol. 4, United Parishes of Whitsome and Hilton. Presbytery of Chirnside, Synod of Merse and Tiviotdale. The Rev. Adam Landels, Minister, William Blackwood & Sons, Edinburgh and Thomas Cadell, London, p. 166 ff.; United Parishes of Swinton and Simprin. Presbytery of Chirnside, Synod of Merse and Tiviotdale. The Rev. James Logan, Minister, p. 187 ff.; Parish of Coldstream. Presbytery of Chirnside, Synod of Merse and Tiviotdale. The Rev. Thomas Smith Goldie, Minister, p. 199 ff.

11. Pont, Timothy 1560?-1614?; Blaeu, Joan, 1596-1673, *Mercia, vulgo vicecomitatus, Bervicensis / auct. Timothei Pont. Merce or Shirrefdome of Berwick,* from *Theatrum orbis terrarum sive Atlas Novus,* Amsterdam: Blaeu, 1654, p. 35, National Library of Scotland

12. Thomson, Rev. James, Minister of Eccles, 'Sketch of the present State of Agriculture in Berwickshire', *Annals of Philosophy; or Magazine of Chemistry, Mineralogy, Mechanics, Natural History, Agriculture, and the Arts,* ed. Thomas Thomson, Vol. I, Number IV, Article III, Robert Baldwin, London, 1813, p. 263

13. Pont, Timothy 1560?-1614?; Blaeu, Joan, 1596-1673, pp. 35-7

CHAPTER 2 – Source to Ravelaw

1. Blackadder, John, fl.1793-1830, map, *Berwickshire,* Imprint [Edinburgh]: s.n., 1797, National Library of Scotland, Shelfmark EMS.s.46

2. *'Old' Statistical Account of Scotland, 1791-99,* Number XIX. United Parishes of Whitsome and Hilton, p. 353

3. Thomson, John, 1777-ca. 1840, Johnson, William, fl. 1806-1840, *Berwickshire,* from *John Thomson's Atlas of Scotland,* imprint, Edinburgh: J. Thomson & Co., 1820, Shelfmark: EMS. S.712(3), National Library of Scotland; Ainslie, John, 1745-1828, *Ainslie's Map of the Southern Part of Scotland,* imprint: Edinburgh: Macreadie Skelly & Co., 1821, Shelfmark: Newman 732, National Library of Scotland; Greenwood, Christopher, 1786-1855, Fowler, William, fl. 1818-1863, Sharp, T., *The County of Berwick,* Shelfmark: EMS.s.322, National Library of Scotland

4. *'New' Statistical Account of Scotland, 1834-45,* Vol. 4, United Parishes of Whitsome and Hilton., p. 169

5. ibid., p. 180

6. *'Old' Statistical Account of Scotland, 1791-1799,* Number Number XIX, United Parishes of Whitsome and Hilton, p. 353

7. Williamson, May G., *The Non-Celtic Place-Names of the Scottish Border Counties,* p. 28

8. Robertson, Lesley A., *Whitsome 1-place study,* latest updates June 2009 (http://homepages.ipact.nl/~robertson/)

NOTES

9. *'New' Statistical Account of Scotland, 1834-1845*, Vol. 4, United Parishes of Whitsome and Hilton, p. 166

10. Mabey, Richard, *Flora Britannica*, Sinclair-Stevenson, London, 1996, pp. 285-6

11. RCAHMS Archaeological Notes, Canmore ID 59738

12. *'New' Statistical Account of Scotland, 1834*, Vol. 4, United Parishes of Whitsome and Hilton, p. 171

13. ibid.

14. RCAHMS Archaeological Notes, Canmore ID 59738

15. RCAHMS Archaeological Notes, Canmore ID 59740

16. For a detailed description of the excavation and findings, see Clarke, Ciara M, Hamilton, Jamie E, with contributions by Bruce, M, Finlayson, B, Hunter, F, Sheridan, A, *Excavation of a cist burial on Doons Law, Leetside Farm, Whitsome, Berwickshire*, Proceedings of the Society of Antiquities of Scotland, Vol. 129 (1999), pp. 189-201

17. ibid., pp. 191-2

18. *'New' Statistical Account of Scotland, 1834-1845*, Vol. 4, United Parishes of Whitsome and Hilton, p. 169

19. RCAHMS Archaeological Notes, Canmore ID 59725

20. Ed. Frances H. Groome, *Ordnance Gazetteer of Scotland: A Survey of Scottish Topography, Statistical, Biographical, and Historical*, Volume VI, Thomas C. Jack, Grange Publishing Works, Edinburgh, London, Glasgow, Aberdeen, 1885, p. 487

21. Fraser, Donald, *The Life and Diary of the Reverend Ebenezer Erskine, A.M. of Stirling, to which is attached A Memoir of his Father, The Rev. Henry Erskine, A.M. of Chirnside*, William Oliphant, Edinburgh, 1831, p. 23

22. ibid., p. 24

23. *'Old' Statistical Account of Scotland, 1791-1799*, Number Number XIX, United Parishes of Whitsome and Hilton, p. 350

24. Robertson, Lesley A., *Whitsome 1-place study*. See The Farms-Ravelaw

25. Clock and Watch Tax Rolls, 1797-8, Vol. 1, National Archives of Scotland, (E326/12); Farm Horse Tax Rolls 1797-8, Vol. 2, National Archives of Scotland, (E326/10)

26. *'Old' Statistical Account of Scotland, 1791-1799*, Number Number XIX, United Parishes of Whitsome and Hilton, p. 350

27. ibid., p. 356

28. Historic Scotland listings: Langrigg (now Ravelaw)-Category C (S), ID 17425, Leetside-Category B, ID 44735

29. *'New' Statistical Account of Scotland, 1834-1845*, Vol. 4, United Parishes of Whitsome and Hilton, pp. 170, 175

30. e.g., Gardner, the Rev. C., 'Spade Husbandry', *The Farmers Magazine*, Volume The First, London, May, 1834, pp. 1-2

CHAPTER 3 – Ravelaw to Swintonmill

1. Williamson, May G., *The Non-Celtic Place-Names of the Scottish Border Counties*, p. 64. For an online Scots/English dictionary, see www.scots-online.org/dictionary

2. *'Old' Statistical Account of Scotland, 1791-1799*, Number Number XIX, United Parishes of Whitsome and Hilton, p. 350

3. *'New' Statistical Account of Scotland, 1834-1845*, Vol. 4, United Parishes of Whitsome and Hilton, p. 170

4. ibid., p. 176

5. *'Old' Statistical Account of Scotland, 1791-1799*, Number Number XIX, United Parishes of Whitsome and Hilton, p. 349

6. *'New' Statistical Account of Scotland, 1834-1845*, Vol. 4, United Parishes of Whitsome and Hilton, p. 170

7. ibid., pp. 174-5

8. ibid., p. 177

9. EEC Ref. No. UK/68/73

10. Blackadder, John, fl.1793-1830, map, *Berwickshire*; Crawford, William & Brooke, William, Map embracing extensive portions of the Counties of Roxburgh, Berwick, Selkirk & Midlothian and Part of Northumberland

11. *'Old' Statistical Account of Scotland, 1791-1799*, Number Number XIX, United Parishes of Whitsome and Hilton, p. 356

12. ibid., p. 350

13. Thomson, John, 1777-ca. 1840, Johnson, William, fl. 1806-1840, *Berwickshire*; Ordnance Survey Six-inch 1st edition, 1843-1882, Berwickshire Sheet XXIII (Inset XXIV), 1862, date of survey 1858, National Library of Scotland

14. *'Old' Statistical Account of Scotland, 1791-1799*, Number XXXVI. United Parishes of Swinton and Simprin, pp. 330-1.

15. ibid., p. 329

16. McKerral, A, *Ancient denominations of agricultural land in Scotland; a summary of recorded opinions with some notes, observations and references*, Proceedings of the Society of Antiquities, Vol. 78, pp. 39-80, 1943-44; see also, Barrow, G. W. S., *The Kingdom of the Scots*, Second edition, Ch. II, 'Rural Settlement in central and eastern Scotland', Edinburgh University Press Ltd., 2003, pp. 233-249

17. *'New' Statistical Account of Scotland, 1834-45*, Vol. 4, United Parishes of Swinton and Simprin, p. 194

18. OS Six-inch 1st edition, Scotland, 1843-1882, Berwickshire, Sheet XXIII (Inset XXIV), Survey date: 1858, Publication date: 1862

NOTES

19. RCAHMS Archaeological Notes, Canmore ID 74694

20. Smith, David B., *Curling Places*, Vol 1, accessed on https://sites.google.com/a/curlingplaces.info/cp/places/0890-swinton

21. Johnston, George, *The Natural History of the Eastern Borders*, Vol. I The Botany, John Van Voorst, London, 1853, p. 194

22. '*New*' *Statistical Account of Scotland, 1834-45*, Vol. 4, United Parishes of Swinton and Simprin, p. 187

23. '*Old*' *Statistical Account of Scotland, 1791-1799*, Number XXXVI. United Parishes of Swinton and Simprin, p. 324

24. RCAHMS Archaeological Notes, Canmore ID 144508

25. Williamson, May G., *The Non-Celtic Place-Names of the Scottish Border Counties*, p. 13.

26. For further information on the Swinton family history and the family trees, see the comprehensive and detailed website of the Swinton Family Society (which has worldwide membership) and particularly the family tree charts, accessible online at www.swintonfamilysociety.org/charts.html

27. For more information, see RCAHMS Archaeological Notes, Canmore ID 59567

28. RCAHMS Archaeological Notes, Canmore ID 144517

29. ibid., Canmore ID 144541

30. ibid,, Canmore ID 144550

31. ibid., Canmore ID 144546

32. Clock and Watch Tax Rolls, 1797-8, Vol. 1, National Archives of Scotland, (E326/12); Farm Horse Tax Rolls 1797-8, Vol. 2, National Archives of Scotland, (E326/10)

CHAPTER 4 – Swintonmill to Charterpath Bridge

1. Scotland's Water Environment Review 2000-2006, Scottish Environment Protection Agency (SEPA), p. 28

2. SEPA Catchment Pollution Reduction Programme under Directive 78/659/EEC on the Quality of Fresh Waters needing Protection or Improvement in order to support fish life: Improvement programme to achieve Guideline values under Article 5 of the Directive, River Tweed Catchment, Monitoring Years: 2005-2007, Section 2

3. ibid., Section 5

4. Kames House including cobbled courtyard, Eccles, Scottish Borders, Category A, listed 9 June 1971, Historic Scotland Building ID: 4115

5. RCAHMS Archaeological Notes, Canmore ID 94666. Also, Scottish Borders, Category A, listed 9 June 1971, Historic Scotland Building ID: 4113

6. ibid., Canmore ID 58523

7. Butrigh House, Eccles, Scottish Borders, Category A, listed 9 June 1971, Historic Scotland Building ID: 4114

8. Milliken, William, Bridgewater, Sam, *Flora Celtica*, Birlinn Limited, Edinburgh, 2004, p. 243

9. *'New' Statistical Account of Scotland, 1834-45*, Vol. 4, Parish of Coldstream, p. 202

10. Kames, Lord Henry Home, *The Gentleman Farmer. Being An Attempt to improve Agriculture By subjecting it to the Test of Rational Principles*, printed for W. Creech, Edinburgh and T. Cadell, London, 1776, pp. 237-50

11. Williamson, May G., *The Non-Celtic Place-Names of the Scottish Border Counties*, p. 43. For an online Scots/English dictionary, see www.scots-online.org/dictionary

12. RCAHMS Archaeological Notes, Canmore ID 59614

13. Williamson, May G., *The Non-Celtic Place-Names of the Scottish Border Counties*, p. 7

14. Gibson, Robert, *An Old Berwickshire Town. History of the Town and Parish of Greenlaw from the Earliest Times to the Present Day*, Oliver and Boyd, Edinburgh & London, 1903, pp. 50-1

15. Williamson, May G., *The Non-Celtic Place-Names of the Scottish Border Counties*, p. 92

16. Muirhead, George, *The Birds of Berwickshire*, Edinburgh: David Douglas, 1895, p. 9 & pp.1-9. A footnote cites Archibald Campbell-Swinton of Kimmerghame's *The Swintons of that Ilk and their Cadets*, July 1883, in connection with the charter

17. RCAHMS Archaeological Notes, Canmore ID 58525

18. *'New' Statistical Account of Scotland, 1834-45*, Vol. 4, Parish of Eccles, Presbytery of Merse and Tiviotdale, the Rev. James Thomson, Minister, p. 52

19. Robertson, Dr. W. H., *A Popular Treatise on Diet and Regimen; intended as A Text Book for the Invalid and the Dyspeptic*, Chatles Tilt, London, 1835, p. 184

20. Coldstream and District Local History Society, Lennel Kirkyard, Headstone Inventory 2, completed Spring 2011. Within Row 4 there are two stones, one erected by Mary Virtue in memory of her husband, Thomas Summerton, aged 46, who died in Berwick in 1824, the other erected to the memory of John Virtue and others. He died in Coldstream on 3 March, 1824 aged 73

21. Forbes, Dr. John, Tweedie, Dr. Alexander, Conolly, Dr. John, *A Cyclopædia of Practical Medicine comprising Treatises on the Nature and Treatment of Diseases, Materia Medica and Therapeutics, Medical Jurisprudence, etc.*, Vol. IV, Sherwood, Gilbert and Piper and Baldwin and Cradock and Whittaker, Treacher and Co., London, 1835, p. 474

22. RCAHMS Archaeological Notes, Canmore ID 58524

23. Braithwaite, Michael, Vice-county Recorder for the Botanical Society of the British Isles, *A Botanical Tour of Berwickshire*, Hawick, 2011

NOTES

24. Johnston, George, *A Botany of the Eastern Borders with the Popular Names and Uses of Plants, and of the Customs and Beliefs which have been associated with them*, John Van Voorst, London, 1853, p. 207. He drew on a fuller description in Hodgson, Rev. John, *A History of Northumberland in Three Parts*, Part II, Vol. II, Newcastle, 1832, p. 458. Holes were drilled into a beech board, the grasses set in to the holes, bound at the rear and cut to size

25. See, for example (but there are others), the Online Scots Dictionary at www.scots-online.org/dictionary/search.asp

26. Williamson, May G., *The Non-Celtic Place-Names of the Scottish Border Counties*, p. 24

27. *Coldstream Cartulary*, Nos. 21, 23, 31, 32, 33, 34, a database accessible online through the *Paradox of Medieval Scotland 1093-1286*, a project funded by the Arts and Humanities Research Council and combining the Universities of Glasgow, Edinburgh and King's College, London (www.poms.ac.uk). See also, Rogers, Charles (ed.), *The Chartulary of the Cistercian Priory of Coldstream with Relative Documents*, Grampian Club, London, 1879, Preface XVI and Abstract of Charters

28. Armstrong, Andrew, 1700-1794, Armstrong, Mostyn, fl. 1769-1791, *Map of Berwickshire*, Imprint: [London]: s.n., 1771, National Library of Scotland

29. Charles I: Translation 1648, 2 March, Edinburgh, Parliament, Parliamentary Register, 18 April 1648 [1648/3/79] NAS. PA2/24, f.18r-24r, accessible online at www.rps.ac.uk/search

30. Dunse History Society, 'The Ainslies', accessible online at www.dunsehistorysociety.co.uk/ainslies.shtml

31. No. 59.—John Ker and H. Gordon Dickson, *Rocheid's Trustees, Pursuers, v. James Russell, Defender*, First Division.—(G.D.F.), 7th December 1838. Recorded in *Reports of Cases decided in the Supreme Courts of Scotland etc. being A Continuation of the Scottish Jurist*, Edinburgh, 1839. pp. 151-3

32. Cooke, G. A., *Topography of Great Britain or British Traveller's Pocket Directory, Vol. XXIV Containing Scotland—General Division, and Northern Division*, Printed for Sherwood, Neely, and Jones, London, p. 3

33. Clock and Watch Tax Rolls, 1797-8, Vol. 1, National Archives of Scotland, (E326/12); Farm Horse Tax Rolls 1797-8, Vol. 2, National Archives of Scotland, (E326/10/2/18)

34. *'New' Statistical Account of Scotland, 1834-45*, Vol. 4, Parish of Coldstream, p. 208; *Collection of the Public General Statutes passed in the Sixth and Seventh Year of the reign of His Majesty King William the Fourth 1836*, printed by George Eyre and Andrew Spottiswoode and published in Numbers by Richards & Co., London, 1836, pp. 668 & 672

35. RCAHMS Archaeological Notes, Canmore ID 59627

36. RCAHMS Archaeological Notes, Canmore ID 59624

37. RCAHMS Archaeological Notes, Canmore ID 293776

38. See www.coldstream-scotland.co.uk/history_castlelaw.html

39. Coldstream and District Local History Society, Lennel Kirkyard, Headstone Inventory 2, completed Spring 2011, Row 1

40. RCAHMS Archaeological Notes, Canmore ID 59637

41. Walker, J. Russel, *Holy Wells in Scotland*, Proceedings of The Society of Antiquities of Scotland, Vol. V, 1882-3, pp. 152-210

42. *Coldstream Cartulary*, e.g. Nos. 15, 16, 17, 18, 19

43. Wildlife and Countryside Act 1981, as amended

CHAPTER 5 – The Hirsel

1. *An Inventory of Gardens and Designed Landscapes in Scotland: Landscape Components*, Historic Scotland, 2007. For additional information see www.historic-scotland.gov.uk/gardenssearchmoreinfo?s=&r=&bool=0&PageID=2079&more_info=Landscape

2. ibid

3. For information on these and other trees, see Chessell, Antony, *The Braw Trees of Coldstream*, Lulu Publishing, 2011 & Rodger, Donald, Stokes, Jon, Ogilvie, James, *Heritage Trees of Scotland*, Forestry Commission Scotland in association with The Tree Council, Edinburgh and London, 2006

4. The Hirsel Site of Special Scientific Interest, Scottish Borders, Site Code: 1532. There is a Citation, a Site Management Statement and a Site Boundary Map. An SSSI is the highest national level of environmental protection and a Special Area of Conservation (SAC) is the highest European level of environmental protection. (www.eservices.ros.gov.uk/ros.sssi.presentation.ui/ros/sssi/presentation/ui/sssi/begin.do)

5. RCAHMS Archaeological Notes, Canmore ID 59635

6. Stoddart, Thomas Tod, *The Angler's Companion   A Popular and Practical Handbook to the Art of Angling*, Third Edition-Revised, Simpkin, Marshall, Hamilton, Kent & Co., London: Thomas D. Morison, Glasgow, 1892, pp.33-4. See also, Stoddart's *The Angler's Companion to The Rivers and Lochs of Scotland*, William Blackwood and Sons, Edinburgh and London, 1847, p. 336

7. Campbell, Dr. R., A Tweed Fisheries Biologist's Week – 9th August 2011, see http://news.rivertweed.org.uk/blog/_archives/2011/8/9/4875475.html

8. For detailed information on freshwater fish in Scotland, see the Scottish Natural Heritage website, www.snh.gov.uk/about-scotlands-nature/species/fish/freshwater-fish

9. Tree planting requirements for the Leet Water were, 50 white willow, 50 grey willow, 50 goat willow, 50 osier, 100 alder, 50 rowan, 50 hawthorn, 50 ash, 50 blackthorn, 50 hazel, 50 oak, 50 d'birch, 50 w'cherry, 50 crab apple, 25 guelder rose, 20 holly, 25 aspen

10. *'New' Statistical Account of Scotland, 1834-45*, Vol. 4, Parish of Coldstream, p. 206

NOTES

11. McIntosh, Charles, *Book of the Garden*, Vol. I, William Blackwood and Sons, Edinburgh and London, 1853, pp. 509-10. Copy of extract and other information provided by Lady Caroline Douglas-Home

12. James VI: Translation 1621, 1 June, Edinburgh, Parliament, Parliamentary Register, 4 August 1621 [1621/6/67] NAS. PA2/20, f.57r-59r, accessible online at www.rps.ac.uk/search

13. Historical Manuscripts Commission, *Report on the Manuscripts of Colonel David Milne Home of Wedderburn Castle*, His Majesty's Stationery Office, 1902, Manuscript 545

14. *Second to None   A History of Coldstream*, Coldstream and District Local History Society, 2010, p. 53

15. Armstrong, Andrew, 1700-1794, Armstrong, Mostyn, fl. 1769-1791, *Map of Berwickshire*, Imprint: [London]: s.n., 1771, National Library of Scotland

16. Cramp, R. and Douglas-Home, C, *New Discoveries at The Hirsel, Coldstream, Berwickshire*, Proceedings of the Society of Antiquities of Scotland, Vol. 109, pp. 223-32

17. RCAHMS Archaeological Notes, Canmore ID 59631

18. Explanatory texts in The Hirsel Museum, situated within the courtyard at the Homestead Visitors' Centre

19. ibid.

20. ibid.

21. www.hirselgc.co.uk

22. RCAHMS Archaeological Notes, Canmore ID 59437; National Museum of Antiquities of Scotland, Accession no.: AF643. See also, 'Donations to and purchases for the Museum and Library, *Proceedings of the Society of Antiquaries of Scotland*, vol. 51, p. 198

23. Syme, David, *Reports of Proceedings in the High Court of Justiciary, from 1826 to 1829*, printed for Thomas Clark, Edinburgh and Saunders and Benning, London, 1829, pp. 188-208 re. Proceedings in the Case of James Craw

24. Williamson, May G., *The Non-Celtic Place-Names of the Scottish Border Counties*, p. 47

CHAPTER 6 – Leet Bridge to Tweed

1. See www.sepa.org.uk/water/river_levels/river_level_data.aspx?sd=t&lc=15013 for the current water level data. Also, click on the National River Flow Archive link to go to the Centre for Ecology & Hydrology station information on flow measurement at www.ceh.ac.uk/data/nrfa/data/station.html?21023

2. Blackadder, John, fl.1793-1830, map, *Berwickshire*, Imprint [Edinburgh]: s.n., 1797, National Library of Scotland, Shelfmark EMS.s.46; Armstrong, Andrew, 1700-1794, Armstrong, Mostyn, fl. 1769-1791, *Map of Berwickshire*, Imprint: [London]: s.n., 1771, National Library of Scotland3. Walker, William, 'Notes on Castle Law

and Lees', *History of the Berwickshire Naturalists' Club*, Vol. XXXIII. 1953, 1954, 1955, printed for the Club, Edinburgh, 1956, pp. 119-121

4. *'Old' Statistical Account of Scotland, 1791-1799*, Number LV, Parish of Coldstream, p. 418. This confirms that, by 1791-1799, The Lees was owned by Mr. Marjoribanks. For additional information see The Clan Pringle website www.jamespringle.co.uk/html/rotp_lees.html

5. See also Obituary of Sir John Marjoribanks, *The Gentleman's Magazine and Historical Chronicle, from January to June 1833, Vol. CIII, Part the First, by Sylvanus Urban, Gent.*, London, 1833, p.371

6. Walker, William, 'Notes on Castle Law and Lees', *History of the Berwickshire Naturalists' Club*, Vol. XXXIII. 1953, 1954, 1955, printed for the Club, Edinburgh, 1956, pp. 119-121

7. ibid.

8. ibid.

9. RCAHMS Archaeological Notes, Canmore ID 83529. Grid Ref. NT84073914. Described in 1980 as an early 19th century T-shaped building measuring about 11.89 m. x 11.14 m. overall, has slit windows, basement area and disused pumps

10. See Fifth Otter Survey of England 2009-2010, Environment Agency. Also, on the Scottish Natural Heritage website at www.snh.gov.uk/about-scotlands-nature/species/mammals/land-mammals/otters/

11. James VI: Translation 1621, 1 June, Edinburgh, Parliament, Parliamentary Register, 4 August 1621 [1621/6/67] NAS. PA2/20, f.57r-59r, accessible online at www.rps.ac.uk/search

12. For a full description and account of the history of Coldstream Priory, see *Second to None A History of Coldstream*, Coldstream and District Local History Society, 2010, Chapter 3

13. RCAHMS Archaeological Notes, Canmore ID 59439

14. ibid.

15. *The Tweed Invasives Project The long-term control of Giant Hogweed and Japanese Knotweed: A case study of the Tweed and practical steps to establishing and delivering a successful, long-term control strategy*, Tweed Forum, 2006

16. For more information on the Scotland River Basin Management Plan, the Solway Tweed River Basin Management Plan and to see copies of the Overview, Chapters 1-5 including appendices, annexes 1, 2 & 3, water body sheets, interactive maps and RBMP data, go to www.sepa.org.uk/water/river_basin_planning.aspx and follow the links. For information on the Tweed Advisory Group and its responsibilities and membership, go to www.tweedforum.org/catchment-management-planning/tweed-aag

Further Reading

Some of the following books are long out of print but can sometimes be bought secondhand or accessed online, even in facsimile format.

1. Braithwaite, Michael, *A Botanical Tour of Berwickshire*, Hawick, 2011.

2. Chessell, Antony, *Coldstream Building Snippets* 'Cans, Quoins and Coursers', Lulu Publishing, London, 2010; *The Braw Trees of Coldstream*, Lulu Publishing, Farnham, 2011.

3. Johnston, George, *The Natural History of the Eastern Borders*, Vol. I The Botany, John Van Voorst, London, 1853.

4. Lang, Andrew & John, *Highways & Byways in The Border*, Macmillan & Co. Limited, London, 1913.

5. Mabey, Richard, *Flora Britannica*, Sinclair-Stevenson, London, 1996.

6. Miles, Archie, *Silva The Tree in Britain*, Ebury Press, London, 1999.

7. Milliken, William & Bridgewater, Sam, *Flora Celtica*, Birlinn, Edinburgh, 2004.

8. Muirhead, George, *The Birds of Berwickshire*, David Douglas, Edinburgh, 1895.

9. Rodger, Donald, Stokes, Jon, Ogilvie, James, *The Heritage Trees of Scotland*, The Forestry Commission in association with the Tree Council, Edinburgh and London, 2006.

10. *Second to None A History of Coldstream*, Coldstream and District Local History Society, Coldstream, 2010.

11. Stoddart, Thomas Tod, *The Angler's Companion, A Popular and Practical Handbook to the Art of Angling*, Third Edition-Revised, Simpkin, Marshall, Hamilton, Kent & Co., London: Thomas D. Morison, Glasgow, 1892; *The Angler's Companion to The Rivers and Lochs of Scotland*, William Blackwood & Sons, Edinburgh and London, 1847.

12. *Wildlife in Britain*, Dorling Kindersley, London, 2008.

Index

Ilustrations in bold.

Map locations not indexed.